MEDICINE THROUGH THE AGES

MODERN MEDICINE

Chris Oxlade

Raintree

Chicago, Illinois

www.capstonepub.com
Visit our website to find out more information about Heinemann-Raintree books.

To order:
☎ Phone 800-747-4992
🖱 Visit www.capstonepub.com
to browse our catalog and order online.

© 2013 Raintree
an imprint of Capstone Global Library, LLC
Chicago, Illinois

Edited by Andrew Farrow, Adam Miller, and Vaarunika Dharmapala
Designed by Philippa Jenkins
Picture research by Ruth Blair
Originated by Capstone Global Library Ltd
Printed and bound in China by Leo Paper Products Ltd

16 15 14 13 12
10 9 8 7 6 5 4 3 2 1

Library of Congress Cataloging-in-Publication Data
Oxlade, Chris.
  Modern medicine / Chris Oxlade.
    p. cm. — (Medicine through the ages)
  Includes bibliographical references and index.
  ISBN 978-1-4109-4646-1 (hb (freestyle)) — ISBN 978-1-4109-4652-2 (pb (freestyle)) 1. Medicine. I. Title.
  R130.O95 2013
  610 — dc23   2011031909

Acknowledgments
We would like to thank the following for permission to reproduce photographs: Corbis pp. 5 (© Mika), 8 (© Salvatore Di Nolfi/EPA), 9 (© Louie Psihoyos), 15 (© Yang Liu), 16 (© Hugh Sitton), 17, 28, 33 (© Bettmann), 20, 24 (© Hulton-Deutsch Collection), 30 (© Najlah Feanny), 31 (© Mike F. Alquinto/EPA), 32 (© John Stanmeyer/VII), 34 (© Stephen Morrison/EPA), 35 (© Reuters), 36 (© Keren Su), 37 (© aman/Demotix), 40 (© Lucas Jackson/Reuters); © Corbis pp. 26, 27; Getty Images pp. 12 (Hulton Archive), 23 (Per-Anders Pettersson), 29 (Marco Di Lauro), 41 (Science Photo Library/Coneyl Jay); Science Photo Library pp. 6 (Zephyr), 7 (Gastrolab), 10 (Jan Halaska), 18 (James King-Holmes), 22 (Andy Crump, TDR, WHO); Shutterstock pp. 11 (© Fanfo), 39 (© Deklofenak); Wellcome Library, London pp. 13, 14, 19, 25, 38.

Cover photograph of *Operation*, 1929 (oil on canvas) by Christian Schad (1894–1982), reproduced with permission of Bridgeman Art Library (© Christian Schad Stiftung Aschaffenburg/VG Bild-Kunst, Bonn and DACS, London 2011).

Every effort has been made to contact copyright holders of any material reproduced in this book. Any omissions will be rectified in subsequent printings if notice is given to the publisher.

Contents

Some words are shown in bold, **like this**. You can find out what they mean by looking in the glossary. You can also look out for them in the "Word Station" box at the bottom of each page.

A Transformation in Medicine

The 20th century was a time of extraordinary change, and this was especially true in the world of medicine. For example, diseases that were killers in 1900, such as polio, were almost wiped out. Hundreds of new drugs were developed. Today's extraordinary surgical techniques, such as heart transplants, would have been unthinkable for a doctor 100 years ago. In 1900, very few people could have afforded to see that doctor. Today, in many countries, people can see a doctor or other health care worker whenever they need to.

This diagram shows the main factors for change that led to improved medicine and health in the 20th century.

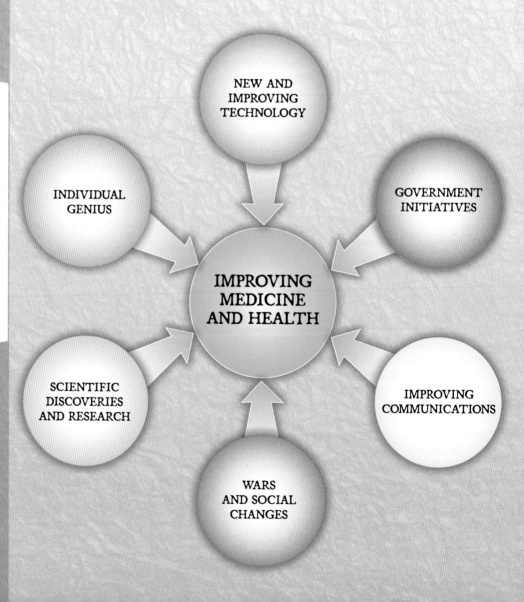

NEW AND IMPROVING TECHNOLOGY

INDIVIDUAL GENIUS

GOVERNMENT INITIATIVES

IMPROVING MEDICINE AND HEALTH

SCIENTIFIC DISCOVERIES AND RESEARCH

IMPROVING COMMUNICATIONS

WARS AND SOCIAL CHANGES

A new approach

At the beginning of the 20th century, doctors used many medical treatments because they thought they worked. There was, however, no real evidence that many of them did. During the 20th century, this changed. Modern drugs and other treatments are now only used after they have been tried out in tests called **clinical trials**. The results from a trial are evidence that the treatments work. This approach is called evidence-based medicine.

Evidence of change

There is plenty of evidence of the success of modern medicine and improvements in public health. Two of the most important pieces of evidence are **life expectancy** and infant mortality. Life expectancy is how long, on average, a person lives. Infant mortality is the number of babies that die before their first birthday, normally shown as deaths per thousand babies born.

Since 1900, life expectancy for men in the United States has increased from 46 years to 75 years. Infant mortality has dropped from 140 deaths per 1,000 births to just 6. It is important to remember, however, that life expectancy and infant mortality have been improved by other factors, too. For example, rising living standards, better nutrition, and cultural changes have also played a part.

 Increasing life expectancy means that many people today enjoy life into their eighties and nineties.

Technical Advances

Today, doctors and nurses use incredible technologies and surgical techniques. These allow doctors to **diagnose** and cure diseases and treat injuries that would have killed people in the past. Faster surgery and less painful recoveries for patients are also possible.

Scanners

Doctors have a range of machines for looking inside patients' bodies. The **ultrasound** scanner was developed in the 1940s. This sends high-pitched sound into the body and builds a picture by detecting echoes. Since the 1960s, the development of babies in their mothers' wombs has been checked with ultrasound. The 1970s saw the development of two new scanners that make highly detailed images of the body. The computed tomography (CT) scanner uses **X-rays** to build images. The MRI scanner uses super-strong magnets to make images. Generally, but not always, CT scanners are used to look at bony structures, while MRI scanners are used to look at soft tissues.

FACTORS FOR CHANGE

COMPUTER POWER

Medical technology such as CT scanners and MRI scanners would not be possible without computers. The development of computers, which began in the 1940s, was an important factor for change in the world of medicine. Today, patients' medical records (details of their past treatments) can be kept on computer for quick reference.

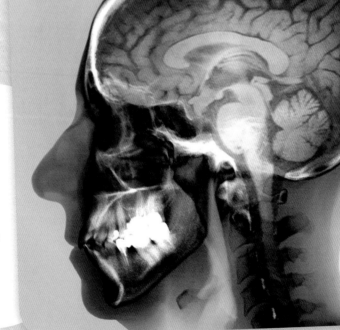

This MRI scan of a patient's brain shows tissues and any possible damage caused to them by disease.

WORD STATION
diagnose identify the nature of a disease or injury through examination

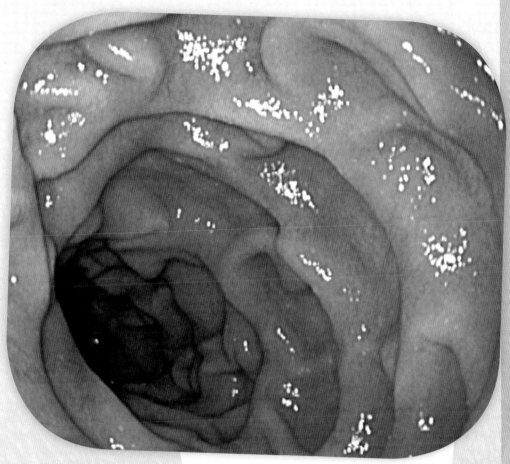

This is a view through an endoscope into a patient's small intestine.

HAROLD HOPKINS
(1918–1994)

Harold Hopkins was a British physicist who improved endoscopes in the 1950s and 1960s. Hopkins worked with surgeons to improve the endoscope. Thanks to Hopkins's discoveries, the endoscope became a far more useful tool. Hopkins also developed better lenses for television cameras.

Endoscopes

An **endoscope** is a device that allows doctors to actually see inside a patient's body. It is a long, narrow tube inserted into the body through an opening such as the mouth. Simple endoscopes were developed in the 19th century, but the images they produced were not very good.

A breakthrough came in the 1950s with the invention of the fibroscope by Harold Hopkins (see the box to the right). It used glass fibers both to illuminate (light up) inside the body and to bring images out.

Keyhole surgery

In **keyhole surgery** (also called laparoscopic surgery), a surgeon inserts surgical instruments into the body through small holes (about half an inch across) in the skin. The surgeon uses an endoscope (see page 7) to see what he or she is doing. Keyhole surgery became widely used in the 1990s. Before then, all operations involved making large incisions (cuts), often through layers of muscle, to reach the site of the operation. This meant more discomfort and longer recovery time for the patient. A more recent development is the use of robots in keyhole surgery. They can position instruments very precisely.

Microsurgery

In the 1960s, surgeons, including Harry Buncke (see the box at left), developed a technique called **microsurgery**. This involves repairing tiny blood vessels and nerves. The surgeon uses a microscope to see what he or she is doing. Microsurgery is used mainly in plastic surgery (reshaping and repairing skin and bone). It even allows surgeons to re-attach fingers, arms, and feet that have been accidentally chopped off!

These surgeons are performing keyhole surgery using a robot. Each arm of the robot is holding an instrument.

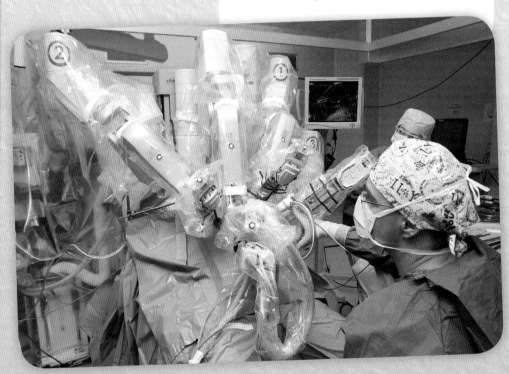

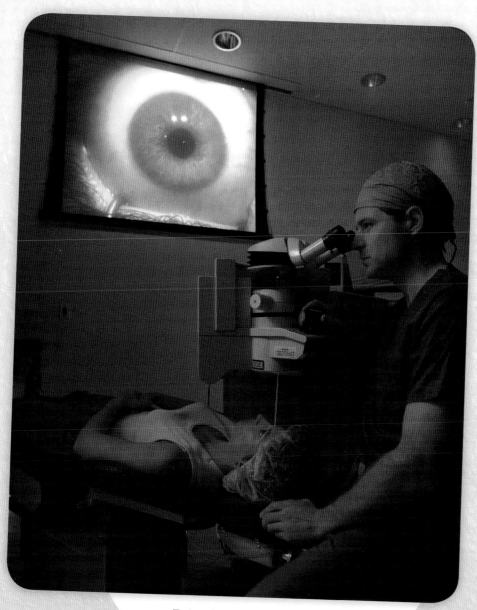

Today, laser eye surgery is an everyday operation.

THE INVENTION OF LASERS

A laser gives off a thin, powerful beam of light. The first laser was built in 1960. Within a few years, surgeons were using lasers in surgery. The laser is one of many examples of how new scientific discoveries and technologies have been applied to medicine.

Laser surgery

The laser scalpel was developed in the 1960s. Surgeons use laser scalpels to slice through tissue and to remove damaged tissues by vaporizing them. Laser scalpels also reduce bleeding from cuts by sealing tiny blood vessels with their heat. The first laser eye surgery was performed in the 1990s. In eye surgery, a laser accurately shapes the **cornea** at the front of the eye to correct the patient's vision.

Mending the heart

Until the middle of the 20th century, heart surgery was almost impossible. Surgeons could not stop the heart to work on it, because this would have killed the patient. In 1953, the first heart operation was performed with the aid of a heart-lung bypass machine, by U.S. surgeon John Gibbon. This machine does the job of a patient's heart and lungs while the heart is stopped. Heart surgery now saves the lives of thousands of people.

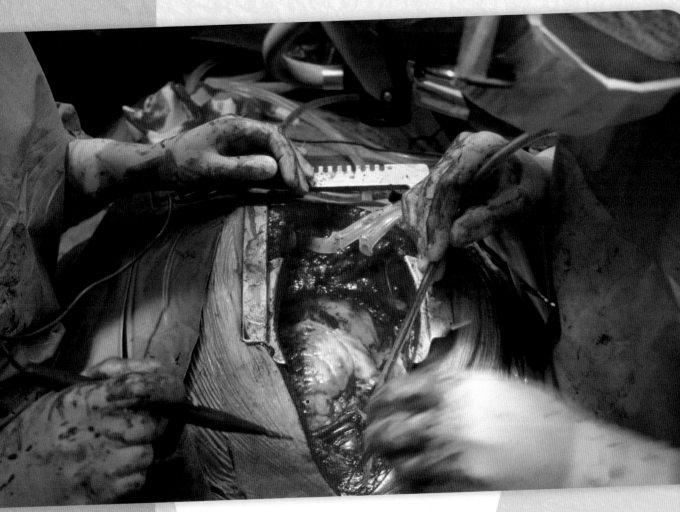

Here you can see open heart surgery in progress. The patient's ribcage has been opened to reveal the heart.

A machine called a defibrillator is used to restart a stopped heart or a heart that is not beating properly. It uses a small electric shock to make the heart muscles beat properly. Portable defibrillators, used in hospitals and ambulances, were developed in the 1960s.

Heart attacks are often caused by blockages in the blood vessels that supply blood to the heart. These are called the **coronary arteries**. In 1964, U.S. surgeon Charles Dotter invented a way to open up the blocked arteries, a procedure known as angioplasty. A thin wire (known as a catheter) with a tiny balloon on the end is pushed along the artery. The balloon is then inflated, which breaks the blockage.

Baby incubators

Babies are sometimes born many weeks before they should be, before their bodies are properly grown. These babies are called premature babies. Today, premature babies are cared for in a **neonatal** intensive care unit, or baby incubator. This machine keeps them warm and feeds them until they are fully developed babies. Even babies that weigh as little as 17.6 ounces (500 grams) can survive. The incubator has saved the lives of thousands of babies. It is one factor in the reduction in infant mortality.

IMPROVING ANESTHESIA

Early **anesthetic** drugs, such as chloroform, had nasty side effects and sometimes caused death. In the early decades of the 20th century, better anesthetic drugs and techniques were developed. These included drugs that were injected instead of inhaled. Anesthesiologists have a range of drugs that are safe for patients and have few side effects. They also use electronic systems to monitor patients while they are "under."

A hundred years ago, this premature baby would almost certainly have died soon after birth.

Transplant surgery

A transplant is an operation in which surgeons replace a diseased or damaged part of a body in one patient (the recipient) with a part from another person (the donor, who has normally died). Kidney, liver, pancreas, heart, lung, and even hand and face transplants are possible today. Thousands of people live today who would have died before transplants were developed. Transplants became possible because of developments in surgery such as microsurgery. The first successful transplant—a kidney transplant—took place in 1954. Kidney transplants have saved hundreds of thousands of lives since.

The first heart transplant operation was performed by Christiaan Barnard in South Africa in 1967. The recipient, Louis Washkansky, survived the operation, but he died 18 days later. The heart came from a young woman.

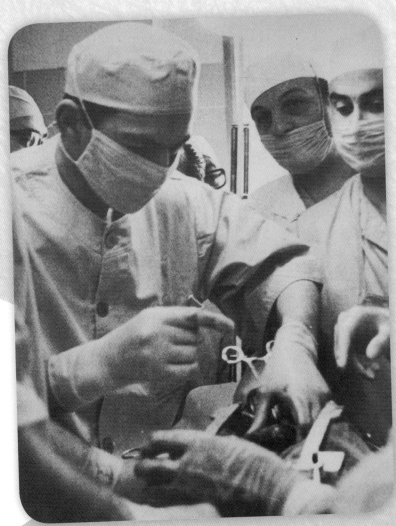

This is Christiaan Barnard practicing his heart transplant surgery on a dog in 1968. This dog did not survive the operation.

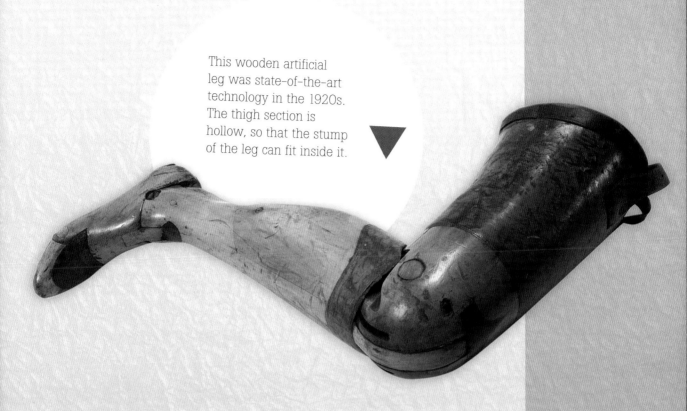

This wooden artificial leg was state-of-the-art technology in the 1920s. The thigh section is hollow, so that the stump of the leg can fit inside it.

A major problem with early transplants was rejection. This happened because a patient's **immune system** treats another person's organ like an infection and tries to destroy it. This problem has been overcome with special drugs. Surgeons gradually learned from both their successes and failures. By the 1980s, patients were surviving for many years with replacement organs.

Artificial body parts

Some damaged or diseased body parts can be replaced by artificial parts. Simple artificial (or prosthetic) limbs, such as false legs, have been around for hundreds of years, but recent advances are dramatic. Artificial arms now have electronics that detect the user's nerve signals, so the user can grip and release objects with the fingers.

Artificial hearts are given to patients who are waiting for a heart transplant. In 1982, the first patient to receive an artificial heart was a U.S. dentist named Barney Clark. Clark lived for 117 days, but he had to be permanently attached to a power supply for the heart. Research continues into developing an artificial heart that can be installed permanently in a patient.

Fighting Disease

Today, we can successfully fight hundreds of illnesses and diseases that were killers at the start of the 20th century. We can do this because, during the 20th century, scientists made many discoveries about how our bodies work. They also discovered how diseases spread and affect our bodies. These findings are the result of medical research. This knowledge has allowed other scientists to develop drugs and other treatments to fight disease.

Synthetic drugs

For hundreds of years, people have known that certain plants help to relieve the symptoms of disease, such as fever and headache. The plants contain chemicals that do the job. In the 19th century, scientists learned how to extract these natural chemicals. They used them to make drugs. In the 20th century, scientists learned how to create **synthetic** drugs, too. Early work on synthetic drugs was carried out by German scientist Paul Ehrlich. In 1910, he made the very first synthetic drug, called salvarsan. Ehrlich made salvarsan to treat a disease called **syphilis**. He experimented with hundreds of chemicals before discovering that salvarsan worked.

Hunt's Remedy claimed to cure "all diseases of the kidneys, bladder, liver, and urinary organs." Today, this boast would need evidence to back it up.

Large-scale factories like this make many drugs today.

THALIDOMIDE

Thalidomide was a drug used as a sedative (to calm down patients). It was first given to patients in 1957. Many pregnant women took the drug. Sadly, thousands of babies whose mothers took thalidomide were born with physical disabilities. This was because the effects of the drug on developing babies were not tested before it was allowed onto the market. The drug company that developed thalidomide provided some help to the surviving sufferers.

Ehrlich also came up with the word *chemotherapy* for fighting disease with chemicals. Doctors now have a vast range of drugs to call on. They prescribe them for fighting diseases and infections, reducing pain, improving digestion, and numerous other jobs.

Developing a drug

By the 1950s, a huge drug-making industry, called the **pharmaceutical** industry, had grown up. Drugs companies design, test, manufacture, and then sell drugs for profit. Making a new drug for a certain job is a long process. Scientists create many different chemicals before deciding which ones to test. The drug is tested in a **clinical trial** to see if it has the desired effect. If it works, the drug must then be approved by the government before being sold.

Vaccines

A **vaccine** is a drug that stops a person from catching a disease. For example, giving a person a measles vaccine makes sure that the person never catches measles. We say it makes them immune to the disease. A vaccine contains a weakened or dead version of the bacteria or **virus** that causes the disease.

Vaccines have been developed for many killer diseases, such as cholera and influenza (flu). Through the use of vaccines, some areas of the world are free of some diseases. An example is polio, which attacks the nervous system. The first polio vaccine was developed by Jonas Salk (see the box at left) and came into use in 1955. Four years later, the number of cases of polio in the United States had fallen by 90 percent. Since then, there has been a worldwide vaccination program against polio. Today, there are just a few thousand cases a year.

JONAS SALK
(1914–1995)

Jonas Salk was a U.S. doctor who made the first successful vaccine for polio. Polio is a disease of the nervous system that, in some cases, can result in muscle paralysis. In the 1940s, Salk worked on flu vaccines, and he then began researching the virus that causes polio. His polio vaccine was made available to the public in 1955.

This baby is being given a vaccine by mouth in order to prevent diseases in later life.

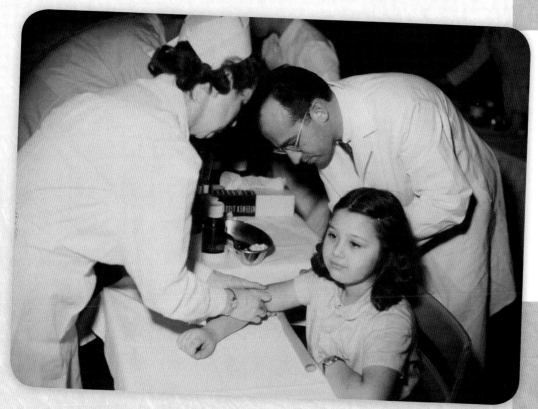

Here, Jonas Salk and a nurse give a polio vaccination to a young girl.

The fight against cancer

Cancer happens when cells in the body start growing out of control. In developed countries, one in three people suffer from cancer at some point in their lives. Since the middle of the 20th century, there have been many advances in **diagnosing** and treating disease (including surgery, radiation therapy, and chemotherapy). Today, although we cannot prevent cancer, people who suffer from it have a much better chance of survival. We also know that the chances of getting certain cancers can be reduced by not smoking and eating a healthy diet.

Mental health

Illnesses that change how people behave are called mental illnesses. Ways of treating mental disease have changed greatly over the last 100 years. In the 1930s, doctors tried electric shock treatment. In the 1940s, they tried a type of brain surgery called lobotomy. In a lobotomy, nerve links in the brain were cut to try to cure certain mental illnesses. Mental patients were sometimes locked away in mental hospitals. From the 1950s, doctors turned to drugs, such as antidepressants, to treat mental illness. We now understand these diseases better, and patients are treated with modern drugs and **psychotherapy**. Even so, mental illness is still not fully understood.

Inheriting disease?

People often think that if a disease has affected their parents and grandparents, then they are likely to inherit the disease. This is true for some diseases, such as Huntington's disease. For most diseases, however, it is a minor factor. It might make it a little more likely that the person will get a disease, but poor diet and lifestyle and lack of exercise can be much more important factors.

Understanding DNA

DNA is a chemical that is found in every cell in your body. DNA is short for "deoxyribonucleic acid." It is an amazingly complicated chemical. It contains a chemical code that controls how a body grows, how it works, and how it fights disease. DNA is passed from parents to children, which is why you have similar characteristics to your parents.

Some diseases are caused by faults in DNA. They include **cystic fibrosis** and **sickle-cell disease**. These diseases can be passed from parents to their children and are known as hereditary diseases. The fact that DNA is responsible for hereditary diseases was discovered in 1943. Another important discovery was the structure of DNA, made by Francis Crick and James Watson in 1953.

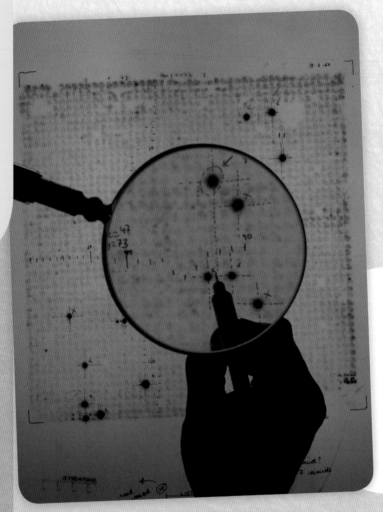

A researcher is examining fragments of DNA during research into inherited breast cancer.

WORD STATION
cystic fibrosis disease that is inherited by children from their parents. It can cause the lungs to become clogged with thick mucus.

Sickle-cell disease is an inherited disease that affects the shape of the blood cells.

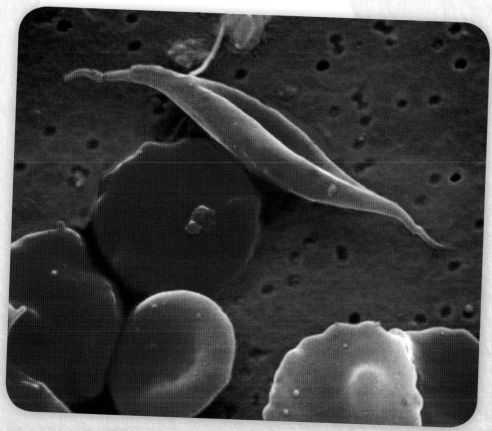

Genes and genetics

A **gene** is a piece of information that is coded in DNA. Different genes control how different parts of your body grow and how they work. For example, one gene controls your hair color, while another gene controls your blood group. Genetics is the branch of science that studies genes. Because some genes are responsible for fighting disease, and faulty genes can cause disease, genetics is a very important area of modern medicine. Doctors can predict if children are likely to suffer from different hereditary diseases in later life.

Public Health

Public health is all about keeping the population of a country healthy. It means making sure people have access to medical care when they are sick. It also means making sure people have healthy homes and are educated about leading a healthy lifestyle (eating healthy food and getting exercise). In the last century, public health has greatly improved.

Housing

In 1900, hundreds of thousands of people lived in overcrowded slums in towns and cities. Whole families were crammed into tiny houses with no fresh water supply and no toilets. These conditions allowed diseases such as typhoid, cholera, and tuberculosis to spread easily. The situation slowly improved through the first half of the 20th century. In the major cities of North America and Europe, many slums were torn down and replaced by new, more spacious housing.

This is Londonderry, Northern Ireland, in 1955. At that time, many people were still living in unhealthy slum housing.

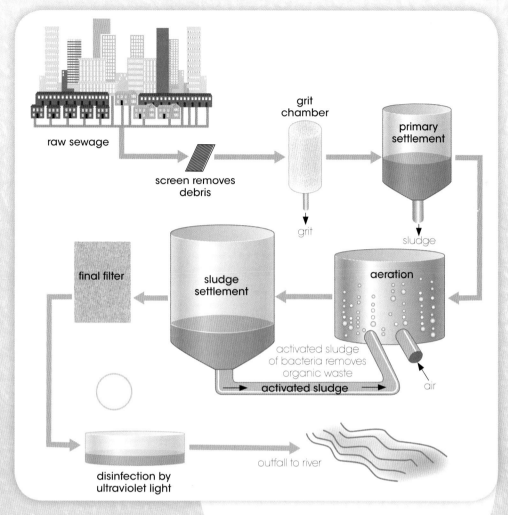

grit
chamber

primary
settlement

raw sewage

screen removes
debris

grit

sludge

final filter

sludge
settlement

aeration

activated sludge
of bacteria removes
organic waste

activated sludge

air

disinfection by
ultraviolet light

outfall to river

These are the processes
that clean sewage at water
treatment plants.

Water supplies and sanitation

Water is very important for people's health. We all need to drink water and wash with water. For people to stay healthy, the water must be clean. Drinking dirty water is a major cause of disease around the world. In the old city slums, lack of **sanitation** meant that local water sources became dirty with human waste. As new houses were built, they were given water piped in from clean water sources, and toilets were connected to sewers to take dirty water away. Sewage treatment plants were built to clean all the dirty water flowing from the cities.

TYPHOID MARY
(c. 1870–1938)

Typhoid Mary, whose real name was Mary Mallon, was at the center of several **epidemics** of typhoid in New York City. In 1904, there was an outbreak of typhoid in an area of New York where Mallon worked as a cook. It was discovered that Mallon had the typhoid bacteria in her body, but she did not suffer from the disease. The disease had spread in the food she handled. In 1907, she was put in an isolation center to stop her from giving the disease to anyone else. She was released after promising not to work as a cook again. In 1914, another outbreak was traced back to her, and she was put in isolation for the rest of her life. In all, she infected 53 people, and three of them died.

Health care for all

At the beginning of the 20th century, many people who were poor and sick had no way to get treatment. A trip to the doctor or a hospital was an expense most could not afford. Government health care for the poor began in the early decades of the 20th century. The first people to be helped were mothers, babies, and young children. However, everyone else still had to pay up or suffer. Then the idea of health insurance was born. In countries such as the United Kingdom, workers who paid a small amount of "national insurance" from their wages each week could see a doctor when they needed. In the United States, private health insurance companies were set up—for those who could afford it.

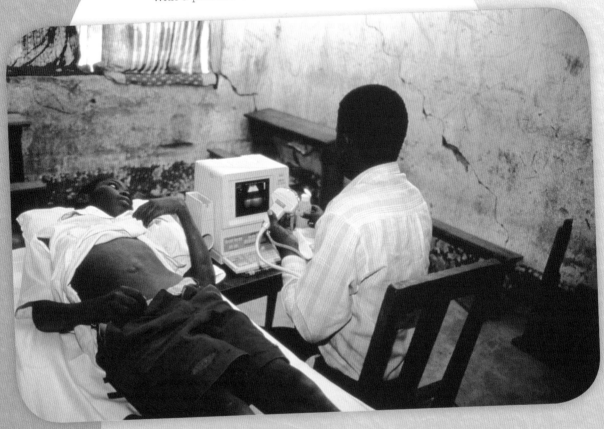

Modern health care is available in developing countries. This patient in Tanzania, Africa, is being examined with a portable **ultrasound** machine.

Medicare and Medicaid

It was not until the 1960s that government health care services were introduced in the United States. Medicare offers treatment for people over 65 years old. Medicaid provides treatment for the poor. But most Americans have private health insurance. Medicare and Medicaid are criticized by many Americans for being inefficient and expensive, yet millions of people rely on them for their health care. They may be cut back in the future.

Today, it is common to see both male and female doctors in a hospital.

WOMEN IN MODERN MEDICINE

In 1900, practically all doctors were men. There were only a handful of women doctors. In the world of medicine, women were seen as caregivers, since they stayed at home. The situation began to change during World War I (1914–1918). There were two factors. First, men were needed to fight the war, and second, more doctors were needed to treat the thousands of wounded soldiers returning from battle. So women trained as doctors. The number of women doctors has slowly increased since. In the United States today, about 30 percent of doctors are women. These numbers are expected to rise.

FITNESS TODAY

These days we eat more fatty foods, such as fast food, cookies, and chips, than people did 100 years ago. People also have less physical jobs. This means that exercise is very important in order to stay fit and healthy.

Diet and fitness

You probably know that what you eat is very important for your health. Food gives your body all the things it needs to grow, to work, and to repair itself. In 1900, people knew that eating certain foods helped to stop them from getting certain diseases, but they did not know why. The mystery was solved by British chemist Frederick Hopkins. He discovered that chemicals called amino acids are needed to stay healthy, and that if you do not get enough of them in your food, you get sick. We now call these chemicals vitamins.

Today, we recognize that getting exercise helps to keep you healthy. Exercise makes your heart muscles work harder, which keeps them strong. Exercise also uses up the energy in some of the food you eat. This prevents you form gaining too much weight, which would be bad for your heart.

The girl on the right is suffering from rickets, a condition in which bones are softened by a lack of vitamin D in the diet. Rickets was common across the world until the early 20th century. It remains a problem in many developing (poorer) countries today.

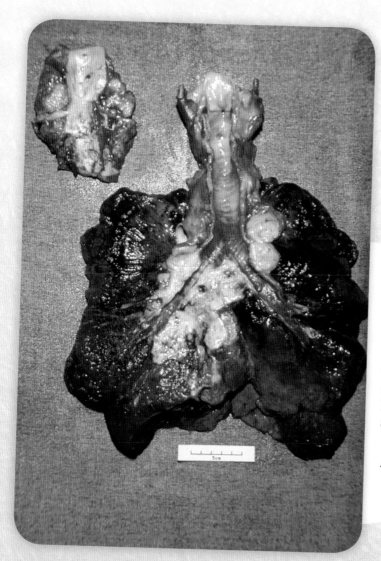

This is a set of lungs taken from a patient who had lung cancer. Healthy lungs are pale and full.

Cause and effect

People often argue about the causes of disease. For example, some people might say that it is safe to smoke. It is okay, they say, because they know people who have smoked all their lives and do not have lung cancer. Even so, they are mistaken. Some people who have never smoked get lung cancer, and some people who have always smoked do not. That is because several factors affect your chances of getting a disease. The fact is that if you do smoke, your chances of getting cancer are much greater.

Educating people about health

Even though we know that a healthy diet and exercise are good for us, many people in developed (wealthy) countries are overweight or obese (seriously overweight). This problem is getting worse—it is known as the obesity epidemic. Many people also smoke, which we know increases the risk of getting cancer and other diseases. That is why governments introduce health campaigns to try to educate people. In 2010 Michelle Obama launched the Let's Move! campaign in the United States, an education program designed to reduce childhood obesity.

The Effects of War

The two world wars were a huge factor in the progress of medicine and health in the 20th century. The main reason for the changes was the need to treat injured members of the armed forces such as soldiers, sailors, and pilots.

Injuries in World War I

New types of weapons were used for the first time during World War I (1914–1918). They included high-explosive shells (which produced flying lumps of metal), poison gas, and heavy machine guns. More soldiers were killed and wounded than in any previous war. Because injuries were so bad, surgeons had to try new techniques. One important technique they developed was the use of skin grafts for burns and other injuries. In a skin graft, surgeons replace damaged skin on part of the body with skin from another part of the body. Surgeons also made advances in brain surgery to treat head wounds, which were very common. After the war ended, surgical techniques were far better than they were when it started.

A soldier wounded in battle during World War I waits on a stretcher to receive treatment.

These U.S. Army medics are performing a blood transfusion during World War II.

Blood transfusions

In a transfusion, a patient's lost blood is replaced by blood from another person (called a donor). Before 1900, many patients died during operations because they lost too much blood. Surgeons tried transfusions, but patients still died. The mystery was solved by Austrian scientist Karl Landsteiner. In 1901, he discovered that mixing blood from two different patients made the blood clot. He found that there are four different types of blood, which he called O, A, B, and AB. A blood transfusion works only when a patient's blood is replaced with blood of the same type. Blood transfusions saved the lives of thousands of soldiers in both world wars.

ERNST CHAIN
(1906–1979)
AND HOWARD FLOREY
(1898–1968)

Ernst Chain and Howard Florey were the scientists who first gave penicillin to a human patient. A few days after World War II began, the UK government made money available for research into penicillin. Chain and Florey, working at Oxford University, in England, got some of the money. They read articles by Alexander Fleming and set to work. It took a long time to grow enough penicillin for their test. After successful tests on mice, they finally gave the drug to a human patient in 1941. The patient, suffering from a terrible infection, quickly improved, but later died after the penicillin ran out.

The story of penicillin

In 1928, Scottish scientist Alexander Fleming had an amazingly lucky accident. Returning to his laboratory after a vacation, he found that a piece of **fungus** had fallen into a dish containing some bacteria. The bacteria around the fungus had died. Fleming identified the fungus as *Penicillium*.

Fleming found that *Penicillium* contains a chemical that kills bacteria. He called the chemical penicillin. He realized that penicillin could be used to fight infections caused by bacteria. He had made the first antibiotic. Fleming could not find a way to make penicillin in large amounts. When World War II (1939–1945) began, scientists realized that the drug would save lives. They found a way to produce it on a large scale.

By 1944, this penicillin factory was sending 15,000 doses a day to sick soldiers.

WORD STATION
fungus organism (living thing) that feeds and grows on organic matter, such as molds, mushrooms, and toadstools

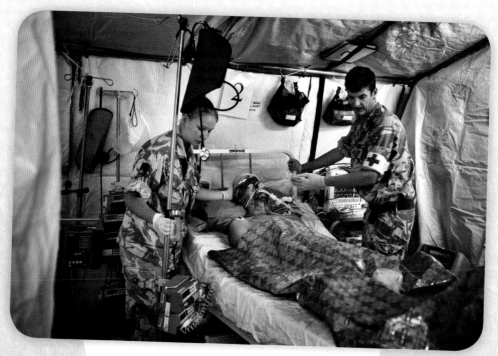

A modern-day field hospital contains state-of-the-art medical equipment.

COMMON CONFUSIONS

Plastic surgery and cosmetic surgery

Plastic surgery reconstructs parts of patients' bodies, usually after they have suffered an injury through a serious accident. Plastic surgery began during World War II, when surgeons began to repair the injured or burned faces of soldiers, sailors, and pilots. Cosmetic surgery is the use of plastic surgery to improve a person's appearance. Many people choose to have cosmetic surgery because it gives them more confidence in their appearance.

By 1944, penicillin was being used on the battlefield. It saved the lives of thousands of soldiers. Penicillin is still a popular antibiotic today.

Wounded at home

Soldiers, sailors, and pilots were not the only casualties of World War II. In the United Kingdom and other countries caught in the war zone, health services had to treat people caught in bombing raids on towns and cities. Health services had to quickly grow and improve to deal with the number of injuries. Many also thought that people who had suffered in the war should have access to health care, which led to many advances in national health care plans.

Global Health Care

Health care is different in every country. Around the world, governments, international organizations (such as the United Nations), charities, and volunteers all have roles in health care. Despite modern drugs and other treatments, some diseases still kill millions of people across the globe.

LIFE EXPECTANCY AND SPENDING

There is a strong link between how much a country spends on health care and how long its citizens can expect to live. Generally, in countries that spend less money, **life expectancy** is shorter. It can be lower than 45 years in very poor countries, such as Afghanistan. In countries that spend more money, life expectancy is longer. However, some countries are exceptions. Cuba spends just $200 per person each year, but life expectancy is 77 years for men and 80 for women. One factor is that the Cuban health care system educates people to prevent disease. Most Western countries spend more than 10 times as much for each person.

Health in developed countries

In most developed (wealthy) countries, there is a mixture of government health care and private health care. People can see a doctor, get emergency medical treatment, and have operations when they need to. Sometimes the treatment is paid for by the government. Sometimes people pay a private health insurance company, which pays for the treatment. In these countries, public health is mostly of a high standard. Most housing is of good quality, and most people have access to clean water and good **sanitation**.

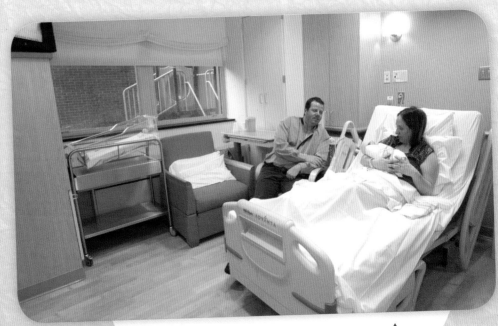

Most patients in developed countries can expect the best medical care in clean, comfortable hospitals.

Health in developing countries

Many economically developing (poorer) countries cannot afford to run government health care programs. Most people have little money and have no access to health care. The sick are helped in their communities or by overseas charities. For most, there is no chance of life-saving surgery for illnesses such as heart failure. Public health is not good, either. In cities, millions live in slums, with no fresh water or sanitation.

Diseases such as cholera and typhoid can spread easily in these conditions, and millions of children die each year from simple problems such as diarrhea. Many people cannot afford to buy healthy food and suffer from diseases caused by a lack of vitamins.

These shanty houses in the Philippines are right next to a filthy river.

So, health care is generally better in the wealthiest countries. However, there are exceptions. The poor in some *developed* countries, such as the United States, have limited access to good health care. Also, the rich in *developing* countries often have access to the latest modern treatments.

Killer diseases

We can now be treated successfully for many diseases that would have killed people 100 years ago. Some diseases have been almost completely beaten by worldwide vaccination and education programs. They include smallpox, polio, measles, mumps, and tetanus. However, some diseases are still killers, because so far we have no drugs or **vaccines** for them.

Malaria is a disease caused by a tiny parasite in the blood that is spread by mosquitoes. It causes fever, headache, and diarrhea, and it often kills. Malaria mostly affects people in tropical countries. In 2008, 243 million people around the world caught malaria, mostly in Africa, and mostly children. A million of them died. On average, malaria kills a child every 30 seconds. Anti-malaria drugs help to stop people from catching malaria, and so can mosquito nets over beds. The mosquitoes that carry the disease can be killed by insecticides. But malaria continues to kill.

This child's mother and grandmother can only wait and hope as he is treated for malaria.

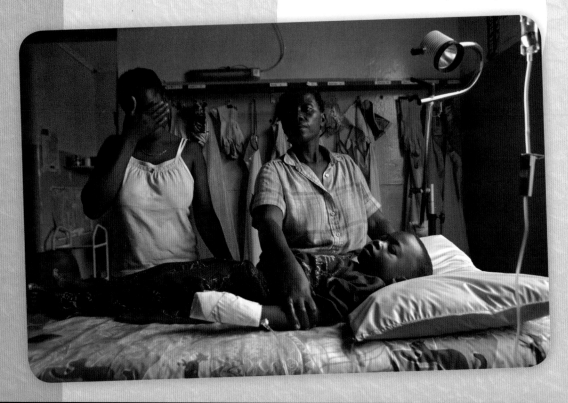

WORD STATION
vaccine substance given to a patient that makes his or her immune system ready to fight a particular disease

Flu epidemics have killed millions of people in the past. Here, masked volunteers hand out food to infected children in 1917.

HIV/AIDS

HIV is a type of **virus** spread by infected blood and sexual contact. It attacks the body's **immune system**, which defends the body against infections. People infected with HIV eventually become sick because of infections. This disease is called AIDS (acquired immune deficiency syndrome). Eventually, these people die. In 2008, 33 million people were suffering from HIV/AIDS, and 70 percent of them lived in Africa. Another 3 million caught it during the year. So far, HIV/AIDS had killed 27 million people.

At the moment, there is no cure or vaccine for HIV/AIDS. Even so, the spread of the virus can be contained through good education, with free condoms being available in many countries. Sufferers can live longer by taking drugs that slow the speed at which the virus reproduces itself. However, the drugs are too expensive for most people, and only 5 million people have access to them.

The World Health Organization

The **World Health Organization** (WHO) is part of the United Nations. The WHO is made up of 193 member countries. It works to improve the health of people all over the globe. This means there is a global approach to health problems, instead of countries working by themselves. The WHO has more than 8,000 experts working for it.

The WHO does many different jobs. It works on the fight against killer diseases, such as HIV/AIDS, tuberculosis, and malaria. It tracks **epidemics** of diseases such as the flu and helps to plan how to stop them from spreading. It organizes worldwide vaccination programs against diseases such as polio. Teams of experts from the WHO are ready to help when there are outbreaks of disease after natural disasters or during wars. The WHO also keeps track of how many people are suffering from different diseases around the world. This data helps countries to plan their health care for the future.

The WHO's most important work is in developing countries. It helps to improve the health of poor people whose governments cannot provide them with health care.

Red Cross workers are unloading food and medical supplies for Kenyans made homeless by a political crisis in 2008.

WORD STATION
epidemic rapid spread of a disease through an area or population

The Smile Train charity carries out surgery on children with cleft palates.

Charities

Charities have an important role in modern medicine. Some charities focus their work on a particular disease. For example, there are charities that raise money to help people suffering from HIV/AIDS and charities that raise money for research into the causes of cancer. Some charities raise money to send medical teams to treat poor people in developing countries or people caught up in natural disasters or wars. Charities can be international, national, or local organizations. For example, local organizations may help their local hospital raise money for a new piece of medical equipment.

Traditional and Alternative Medicine

For thousands of years, people have used plants to treat infections, diseases, and symptoms such as pain and fever. These traditional medicines were discovered over time, probably by accident. In the last few decades, similar sorts of treatments that do not rely on modern drugs or high-tech equipment have become popular in the West. These treatments are known as alternative medicine.

Traditional medicines

Traditional medicines (also known as indigenous medicines) are used by millions of people around the world. This is often the case in places where modern medicines are unavailable or are too expensive. Sometimes people do not trust modern medicine and would rather use medicines that their parents used. In some countries, 80 percent of people rely on traditional medicine. Some traditional medicines are also used as alternative medicines in the West.

Many modern medicines are substances that come from plants or are copies of substances from plants. An example is the painkiller aspirin, which originally came from a plant called white willow. This plant had been used for centuries to treat pain and fever.

MEDICINES FROM PLANTS

Here are some examples of modern drugs that were originally found in plants.

- *Aspirin:* This is a form of salicin, which was found in willow bark. It is used for the relief of pain and fever.
- *Quinine:* This is found in the bark of the cinchona tree. It is used to prevent and treat malaria.
- *Digitalis:* This is found in the foxglove. It is used for the treatment of heart conditions.

Here you can see all sorts of traditional medicines for sale in a market stall in China.

This rhinoceros has been killed for its horns. Some people believe rhino horns have medicinal properties.

Is natural safe?

Many people think that because traditional herbal medicines are natural, they must be safe to use. This is not always true. Some herbal medicines can be harmful to some people, perhaps because of an allergic reaction. They can also interfere with modern drugs if the two are taken together.

Controversial medicines

Some traditional medicines are controversial today. For example, some use ingredients from endangered animals in their preparation, including the tiger, sea horse, and rhinoceros.

Rhinoceros horn is used in many countries, including China, India, and Malaysia. The horn is ground up and mixed with boiling water to make a medicine that people believe will cure all sorts of complaints, from fever to snakebites. But so many rhinoceroses have been illegally hunted for their horns that their numbers have dramatically declined. There is no scientific evidence that this medicine works, and activists around the world are trying to convince people not to buy products containing rhino horn.

Alternative medicine

In Western countries, many people use "alternative" or complementary medical treatments, such as homeopathy or acupuncture. These treatments do not use modern drugs or surgical techniques. Some treatments that are thought of in the West as alternative treatments actually just come from other countries, where they are everyday treatments that have been popular for centuries. Yoga is an example. It originated in India more than 6,000 years ago. Although most Western people practice yoga as a form of relaxation, some believe it prevents some illnesses. Other alternative treatments have been developed in the last few decades.

Acupuncture involves pushing very thin needles into specific locations on the body.

THE PLACEBO EFFECT

Doctors and scientists think that many alternative therapies work for some patients because the patients think they will work. A therapy works because the patient believes in it, and not because it has any physical effect. This is known as the **placebo effect**. Placebo medicines, which contain no drugs at all, are often used in clinical trials.

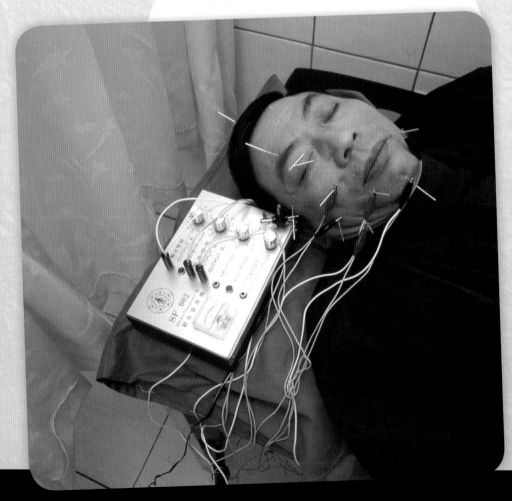

Many people think that yoga and meditation can help prevent disease.

At first, doctors and other medical professionals were suspicious and skeptical about all alternative medicine. This was because alternative medicines are not backed up by scientific evidence or **clinical trials**. Also, the therapists who practiced them did not have medical training. More recently, some doctors have accepted that some treatments, such as acupuncture, work for some patients.

Popular alternative medicines

- *Homeopathy:* This is based on the idea that if taking large amounts of a chemical gives a person the symptoms of a disease, taking a tiny amount of the same chemical will cure the disease. Homeopathy was founded by German doctor Samuel Hahnemann (1755–1843). There is no scientific evidence that it works.

- *Chiropractic:* This was founded by a U.S. doctor named Daniel David Palmer (1845–1913). Chiropractors believe that some illnesses and diseases are caused by bones pressing against nerves in the spinal column. They bend and twist the spine to try to cure problems. There is evidence that some patients benefit from this treatment.

- *Reflexology:* This is based on the idea that massaging the feet in certain places can help cure some medical conditions. It was developed in the 1930s by Eunice Ingham. There is little scientific evidence that this is effective.

Where Are We Now?

Medicine has come a long way since the early 20th century. Thanks to discoveries and research, our knowledge about how the human body works and how diseases affect it has greatly improved. We have new drugs, such as antibiotics, to fight disease. Complex operations that were out of the question a century ago, such as eye surgery and organ transplants, are routine today. A person who gets sick today has a far better chance of surviving than a person who got sick in 1900. Public health has improved, so people are less likely to catch diseases in the first place.

It is not all good news, however. Despite all these advances, there are still diseases that we do not know how to treat, or even if we will ever be able to, such as cancer and HIV/AIDS.

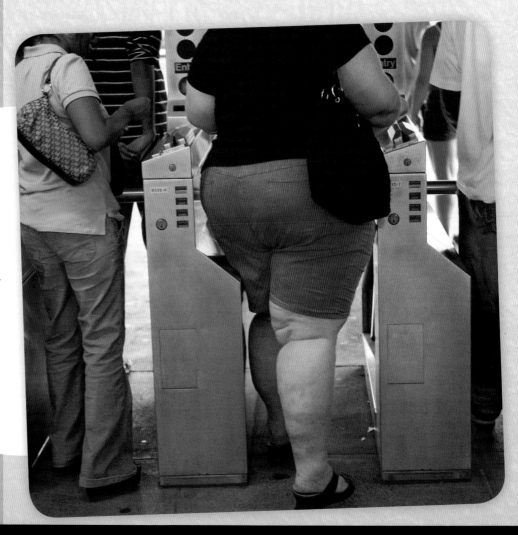

Obesity is a new health problem facing many people today. It is common in Western countries.

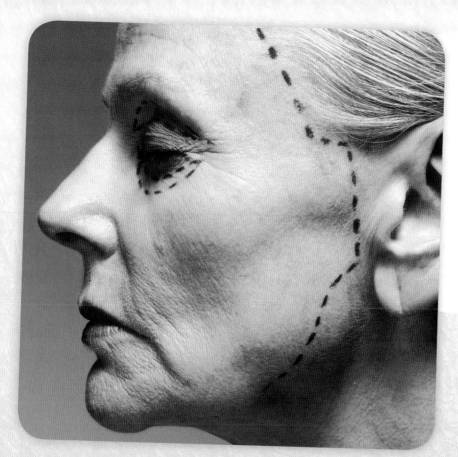

Medicine is increasingly being used to alter a person's appearance.

On the horizon

Researchers are studying cells called **stem cells**. These can grow into any sort of cell, such as nerve cells, blood cells, and skin cells. Stem cells could be used to regrow or repair parts of the body. For example, growing brain cells from stem cells may help sufferers of **Alzheimer's disease**. However, the use of stem cells is controversial. Some stem cells used for experimental treatments are gathered from human **embryos**, which some people think is wrong.

The future

If the pace of change continues as it has over the last 100 years, it is hard to imagine what the world of medicine will be like at the end of the 21st century. What discoveries might we make about the human body? Will we overcome current problems such as cancer? New diseases may appear to challenge us—especially as increasing global travel and the effects of climate change mean that diseases will find new places to thrive. Perhaps the best change of all would be equal access to health care for everybody on the planet.

FACTORS FOR CHANGE

NEW PROBLEMS

A new factor for change is the increasing lifespan of people in developed countries. Better medicine has allowed people to live longer, but with old age comes new problems. Many people who live into their eighties and nineties suffer from failing joints and dementia (impaired brain function that causes memory loss and personality changes). Medicine has to respond to these new challenges.

Timeline

1900	Access to health care is limited for most people in the world
1901	Austrian scientist Karl Landsteiner discovers that there are several different types of blood (later called blood groups)
1910	German scientist Paul Ehrlich develops the first **synthetic** drug, called salvarsan
1914–1918	World War I
1918	A flu pandemic kills between 50 and 100 million people worldwide
1927	The first **vaccines** for the diseases tuberculosis and tetanus are developed
1928	Scottish scientist Alexander Fleming discovers penicillin, the first antibiotic
1930s	Private health insurance companies start to develop in the United States
1938	Typhoid Mary, who was the source of several typhoid outbreaks, dies at age 68
1939–1945	World War II
1940s	The **ultrasound** scanner is developed
1944	Penicillin saves the lives of thousands of soldiers fighting in World War II
1945	The first vaccine for the flu is developed
1948	The **World Health Organization** (WHO) is formed
1950s	British physicist Harold Hopkins invents the fibroscope, a flexible **endoscope**

1953	Francis Crick and James Watson discover the structure of **DNA**. U.S. surgeon John Gibbon uses a heart-lung bypass machine during surgery for the first time.
1955	A vaccination against polio, developed by U.S. doctor Jonas Salk, comes into use
1957	The drug thalidomide is given to patients for the first time
1960s	Medicare and Medicaid are set up in the United States. The portable heart defibrillator is developed. The checking of babies before birth using ultrasound scanners begins.
1964	U.S. surgeon Charles Dotter invents angioplasty for clearing blocked **coronary arteries**
1967	South African surgeon Christiaan Barnard performs the first heart transplant operation
1969	U.S. surgeon Harry Buncke performs the first operation to use **microsurgery**
1970s	The computed tomography (CT) scanner is developed. The magnetic resonance imaging (MRI) scanner is developed.
1978	Louise Brown, the first "test tube" baby, is born in England
1980	The disease smallpox is believed to have been ended
1983	HIV, the disease that causes AIDS, is identified
1990s	The first laser eye surgeries are performed
1996	Dolly the sheep, the first mammal to be cloned, is born
2003	The Human Genome Project is completed
2008	More than 33 million people around the world suffer from HIV/AIDS

Glossary

Alzheimer's disease form of mental deterioration that can occur in middle or old age, resulting in memory loss, personality changes, and impaired judgment

anesthetic substance used in operations to stop a patient from feeling pain

clinical trial series of experiments designed to test how well a new drug or new medical technique works, and whether it is safe for patients

cornea transparent layer at the front of a person's eye, which can become opaque (not able to be seen through) because of certain illnesses

coronary artery large blood vessel that carries oxygenated blood to the heart muscles

cystic fibrosis disease that is inherited by children from their parents. It can cause the lungs to become clogged with thick mucus.

diagnose identify the nature of a disease or injury through examination

DNA short for "deoxyribonucleic acid," the complex chemical that holds the information contained in a person's genes

embryo unborn baby, before the stage when its organs have developed (normally before it is eight weeks old)

endoscope medical instrument that can be inserted into the body and allows doctors to see inside their patients

epidemic rapid spread of a disease through an area of population

fungus organism (living thing) that feeds and grows on organic matter, such as molds, mushrooms, and toadstools

gene piece of information stored in cells that passes hereditary information from parent to child

immune system system that fights infection in a person's body

keyhole surgery surgery that is carried out through a very small cut in the body

life expectancy average age that men or women live to in an area, given in years

microsurgery surgery carried out on very tiny structures in the body, with the aid of specialized instruments

neonatal relating to newborn children

pharmaceutical relating to medicines, their use, and their manufacture

placebo effect benefit from a treatment that occurs because the patient believes in it

psychotherapy treatment of mental problems by talking about problems with an expert

sanitation systems that bring fresh water to people and take away and clean sewage

sickle-cell disease disease in which red blood cells are distorted, so that they cannot carry oxygen efficiently

stem cell cell that can change into any sort of cell in a human body, such as a blood cell, nerve cell, or skin cell

synthetic artificial

syphilis sexually transmitted disease that can infect the skin, bones, muscles, and brain

ultrasound sound of extremely high frequency (too high for humans to hear). Ultrasound is used to look at babies inside the mother's womb.

vaccine substance given to a patient that makes his or her immune system ready to fight a particular disease

virus tiny particle that invades cells and multiplies in them

World Health Organization (WHO) group within the United Nations that works to improve global health through research and technical support

X-ray type of radiation that passes through soft tissue but not bone and is used to see structures inside the body. It is also the name of an image taken with X-rays.

Find Out More

Books

Clayborne, Anna. *What Are the Limits of Organ Transplants?* (Sci-Hi: Science Issues). Chicago: Raintree, 2012.

Fullick, Ann. *Medical Technology* (Sci-Hi: Science and Technology). Chicago: Raintree, 2012.

Hartman, Eve, and Wendy Meshbesher. *The Scientists Behind Medical Advances* (Sci-Hi Scientists). Chicago: Raintree, 2011.

Lovegrove, Ray. *Health: Ethical Debates in Modern Medicine* (Dilemmas in Modern Science). Mankato, Minn.: Smart Apple Media, 2009.

Vickers, Rebecca. *Medicine* (From Fail to Win!). Chicago: Raintree, 2011.

Web sites

kidshealth.org/teen/your_body/medical_care/alternative_medicine. html
Learn more about alternative medicine at this web site.

www.knowitall.org/kidswork/hospital/history/modern/index.html
This history of medicine includes facts about modern medicine.

www.letsmove.gov
This is the official web site of Michelle Obama's Let's Move! campaign.

www.who.int
Visit the official web site of the World Health Organization to find out about the work the group does and some facts about contemporary health issues.

More topics to research

Try researching further into some of the topics that you have read about in this book. Is there a particular theme that interests you? Here are some ideas to get you started:

- the history of Medicare and Medicaid

- the effect of air pollution from burning fuels on people's health, especially in cities

- the spread of malaria, and what effect climate change is having on this

- finding a clean water supply in developing countries, and the role of charities such as WaterAid

- the effect of shell shock on the soldiers of World War I

- the work of the World Health Organization

- look at graphs of how life expectancy and infant mortality have changed since 1900

- robots in the operating room

- the rise of modern diseases such as diabetes

- the ethical debate over the use of embryonic stem cells

- The cover of this book shows a detail from the painting *Operation* by Christian Schad. What does it tell you about medicine in the modern age? The surgeons are wearing gloves and using metal instruments. Do you think this might have been different in the past? If so, how?

Index

crowd breakers & mixers

& MIXERS

THE ideas LIBRARY

R YOUTH GROUPS

crowd breakers

breakers

& MIXERS

THE *ideas* LIBRARY

R YOUTH GROUPS

Crowd breakers & Mixers 2

Copyright © 2003 by Youth Specialties

Youth Specialties Books, 300 South Pierce Street, El Cajon, California 92020 are published by Zondervan Publishing House, 5300 Patterson Avenue Southeast, Grand Rapids, Michigan 49530

Library of Congress Cataloging-in-Publication Data

Crowd breakers and mixers 2.-- 1st ed.
        p. cm. --   (Ideas library)
    ISBN 0-310-25051-X (pbk.)
    1.   Christian education of young people.   I. Title: Crowd breakers and
mixers two. II. Youth Specialties (Organization) III. Series.
    BV1485.C76 2003
    268'.433--dc21

                                                        2003004262

Web site address listed in this book are current at the time of publication. Please contact Youth Specialties by email (YS@YouthSpecialties.com) or by postal mail (Youth Specialties, Product Department, 300 South Pierce Street, El Cajon, California 92020) to report URLs that are not operational and to suggest alternate URLS if available.

Illustrations by José Traghetti

Edited by Rick Marschall and Linda Bannan
Production assistance by Nicole Davis
Content editing by Roni Valerio-Meek, Sarah Sheerin, and Steve Case
Proofreading by Linnea Lagerquist

Interior and cover design by Mark Rayburn

Printed in the United States of America

05 06 07 08 09/ VG /10 9 8 7 6 5 4

Table of Contents

7

MIXERS

THE *ideas* LIBRARY

Toilet Paper Confessions

This game requires only toilet paper. Have your group sit in a circle and pass the roll to each member. Tell them to place the roll on their finger and see how many tissues they can get by pulling on the paper once. After everyone takes a turn, then have the players count how many tissue squares they got. Then, they must tell you one thing about themselves for each tissue they got. *John Cook*

Move Your Buns

You need multiple rows of chairs for this game, with an aisle down the center. Split your group into two or four teams—one team sitting on the left and one on right. (If you have four teams, put two teams on each side.) The leader makes statements like these—

- If you are wearing shoes...
- If you were ever a cheerleader...
- If you have brown hair...
- If you had a big zit in the last week...

If the question is true of the student, he must move down the row. (For example, the team sitting in the chairs with the aisle on their right will move to the right on each turn.) Students move one spot for each question that is true for them. If someone is sitting where a student moves, she sits on that person's lap or squeezes onto the same chair. The first team to get all of its members on one side wins. *Amy Cole*

Telephone Pictionary

You need two teams of at least 15 people each; fewer are okay, but this minimum number is best. Line up 10 students from each team and put the rest in a group across the room. Whisper a sentence or statement to the first person in line. That student whispers it to the next person in line and so on, just like a normal game of Telephone. When the last person in line has heard the statement, he runs across the room to the rest of his group and starts drawing images and pictures to get the group to say the statement he heard. (Players can't use letters or numbers in their drawings.)

VARIATION—Draw a fairly simple picture and show it to the last person in line.

Then, as in Telephone, that person uses his finger to draw the picture on the back of the person in front of him, and that person draws what she felt on the back of the person in front of her, and so on until it gets to the first person in line. Then the first person in line draws what he felt on a piece of paper, intending that it is what the original picture was. The closest drawing wins.   *Amy Cole*

By the Way

You can do this activity anytime and anywhere. Have everyone sit in a circle. Go around the circle and have each person say her name and add, "by the way" plus a four-word phrase that describes something about them. For example, "My name is Pat and *by the way* my cat is fat." As they move around the circle, each person must repeat what all of the previous people said so that they get to know each other better. This game is really funny because the students get really creative about what they say and how they say it.   *Heath Kumnick*

Mystery Punch

In this fun mixer (Get it? Mixer?), students work in small groups, create, and laugh a lot.

You need a variety of mixing supplies: fruit juices, chocolate syrup, fruits, soda—the more creative the better. If you avoid things like pickle juice and sour milk, you can use these drinks with your supper. Be creative without being disgusting. The Aztecs had a beverage called Chocal. The closest thing to recreating it today would be chicken broth, cocoa, and Tabasco sauce. (Don't make that face; it's pretty good!)

Tell the groups to create their own commercial beverage. They can name it and come up with a slogan. After a given time limit, have the groups share what they've come up with. Have lots of Dixie Cups so that everyone can try all of the drinks. Give prizes for Best Name, Worst Looking, and Best Tasting.
NOTE—This game also works with pizza!   *Becky Carlson*

Silly Putty Body of Christ

This is an object lesson that emphasizes the importance of being part of a group—the body of Christ (unity building, giving, and receiving, 1 Corinthians 12:12-26). First, you need Silly Putty or Play-Doh for everyone in the group. The Silly Putty should be different colors. Youth love to play with Silly Putty, and they like to get things free! Have each one mold the Silly Putty into a symbol of who they are. Give them a chance to share what they made and how it represents who they are. After each person shares, explain that it is nice to be recognized as individuals and each individual helps make up the group; but to become part of a group, you have to give of yourself.

Let them have a reflective opportunity to give back to the group in a symbolic way by giving back the Silly Putty. As the youth give back the Silly Putty, clump it all together in a big ball. DO NOT MIX IT TOGETHER. The result is one big, colorful ball of Silly Putty. The big ball represents the members of the group, each one bringing something unique to the group to create something beautiful. Then comes the fun part—point out that as we give of ourselves, we also receive. Give a piece of the big ball to everyone who gave his Silly Putty. Let students know they have bit of everyone in their new piece of Silly Putty. They each take home a piece of the group!

NOTE—
You can't take yourself out of the group once you've "given" yourself. If you try, your Silly Putty sticks to the others.

Once each person has her piece, it is beautiful to see all the different colors. But if you keep kneading the putty, it soon becomes one new, not-so-beautiful color.

Jeanne Wong

Stick-on Name Badges

Prepare in advance as many stick-on name badges as you will have participants. Use names from themes such as nursery-rhyme characters, children's story characters, TV characters, TV and/or movie celebrities, or professional athletes. As students arrive, place a badge on each person's back and tell them the theme. Each person must figure out who she is by introducing herself to another member of the group and asking only one yes-or-no question. When people figure out who they are, they move their name badges to the front; but they remain in the game to answer questions of those still trying.

Don Mullins

Name Crowd Breaker

Here's a quick get-to-know-the-names game. Start by sitting on the floor in a circle. Go around the circle with each person saying his name three times. The group responds each time with, "Who?" The speaker usually gets louder each time but given the opportunity to be creative, students have a lot of fun with this. Some students say their name slower or quieter or weirder each time. A sample would go like this: The first person introduces himself in a normal tone of voice, "Mike." The group responds with, "Who?" Mike repeats a little louder, "MIKE!" The group asks again, "Who?" This time Mike yells at the top of his voice, "MIKE!" And then the group says, "Ohhhh, Mike." Then it's the next person's turn.   *Tim Bilezikian*

The Think-like-Me Game

Make a sheet of goofy sentences, and pass them out to your group. Give students 30 seconds to fill in the blanks. When the leader says, "GO!" students start looking for other students who wrote the same answer. When they match, they sign one another's paper. Here are some ideas to get you started.

🡒 Gabe's dog is so big, instead of a stick he fetches a _____

🡒 It's going to be so cold on the camping trip next month that Laura is going to get frost on her _____

🡒 Every time I look at whipped cream I think of

_____

🡒 You may not believe in reincarnation but in a past life (youth director) was

_____

🡒 Very few people appreciate a dessert topping made entirely out of

_____

🡒 "This fruit juice tastes funny," said Bill, "It's like they squeezed a

_____

to get it."
Everett Bracken

Capital Letter

Before the meeting, write one capital letter on as many stick-on name badges as there are participants. Place a badge on the back of each person in the group, and give each player a pencil and piece of paper. Each person must figure out what letter is on his back by introducing himself and saying a five-letter word. The other person indicates whether or not the word contains the letter on the first person's back. By keeping track of the words that do and do not contain the letter, a person can eventually figure out the letter that is on his back. When people figure out their letters, they move their badges to the front, but remain in the game to answer questions from those still trying to figure out what their letters are.
Don Mullins

Who Are U 2?

Have the students pair up with someone they don't know or someone they feel is very different from them. Each pair must find five things they have in common and write these down on a sheet of paper. When all of the groups finish, an adult leader reads the lists, and the group must decide which pair the sheet belongs to. (NOTE—The pair that knows their list is being read should try to throw off the rest of the group by guessing too. If they just sit there and smile it's sort of a giveaway.)

Christy Dixon

Seeking My Fortune

Here's a great mixer for small groups. Buy a box of fortune cookies, and replace the fortunes with slips of paper that contain the spiritual gifts Paul writes about in Romans 12:4-8. (Put one gift on each slip.) Pass these out to your group. Then have each student break open a cookie and read the gift on the slip. Have students explain to the group how this gift applies to them or how they can use this in everyday life. After the students read their slips, let them trade their slips for ones they feel are closer to what they think their gifts really are. Go around the circle and ask them to explain why they traded.

VARIATION—if you have some comic-book fans in your group, try this game after watching a clip from the movie *X-Men*. What are your students' powers?

VARIATION—You can also put the slips into balloons and blow them up. Students pop a balloon to reveal their gifts. Talk about how God wants us to explode with the gifts we are given and not just slowly let the air out. *Steve Case*

GUMP-isms

Play the clip from Forrest Gump where Tom Hanks says, "My momma said life is like a box of chocolates..." Have your group come up with as many Gump-isms as they can. Give a box of chocolates to the best one or the most bizarre.

Steve Case

More in Common than a Cold

This game works best in large groups. Have students introduce themselves to someone in the crowd. Next, have them find something they have in common in one of these five categories: favorite food, favorite band, favorite TV show, favorite movie, and favorite sport. When they find someone they have a match with, they must stay together, find another pair, introduce themselves, and find a way to link up with the other two. Those four then find another group of four and so on and so on.

Dave Fox

The Reason for Extinction

You need paper, crayons, markers or pens to draw and color with, and a list of fake animal names and attributes.

Divide the students into a few teams, and distribute the paper and drawing implements. Read the name of a fake animal and a couple of its attributes, (it can fly, or swim, it eats meat, it eats berries, has claws, or how big it is). Do this with each team. Then give them about five or six minutes to draw the animal as a team. Have students take turns as the official artist within each team, and play until everyone has a chance to add to the drawing. Then have sponsors judge each picture using categories such as most imaginative, most accurate, and best artwork.

Brian Stegner

Whozat?

Before the game find out one fact about each student. Print these facts on a sheet of paper, then make copies and pass them out. Turn the students loose and have them find out which student belongs with what fact.

Here are some ideas for facts: favorite song; what father does for a living; what mother does for a living; favorite pizza topping; and poster on bedroom wall.

Joel Lusz

Ten Questions

First have students team up with someone they know well or fairly well. Next, ask each team of two to team up with another pair that they don't know well or at all. Now each group should have four people in it.

Beginning with the person in each group who has the most money in their pocket, play 10 Questions, a modified form of the game 20 Questions. (Remember, in this game players can only ask yes or no questions!)

The first player's topic is—The person (living or dead) I would most like to have lunch with.

After two minutes call Time and ask each group to question player #2 (the person to the left of player #1). Player #2's category is—The first thing I would wish for if I had Aladdin's lamp (excluding more wishes or money).

Continue play until each group member has been questioned about her category. Player #3's category is—The historic event I would most like to witness (if I had a time machine).

Player #4's category is—An event in my own life I would like to relive. *Len Woods*

End-of-School Blowout

This crazy discussion mixer gives small to medium-sized groups a chance to have fun and get better acquainted. It takes about 10 minutes. Use this mixer on or near the last day of school.

Ask everyone to pair up, and then give each pair a copy of the sheet on page 18. It is self-explanatory.

NOTE—for older groups, change the last statement to "make predictions about what you'll all be doing five years from now."
Len Woods

Mixed-Up Name Game

Have your students introduce themselves, only they must pronounce their names backwards. For example, if my name were Fred Bruffel, I would actually say *Derf Leffurb*.

For those students with long last names, help by writing down the name in reverse as they spell it to you correctly.

This game gets quite a few laughs, and it may actually start some new nicknames for some of the students. The best part is, while students concentrate on saying the names in reverse, it helps their normal names stick in your mind. *Brant Taylor*

Not Just Any Game

This is a fun mixer to do with junior high students. Photocopy the sheet on page 21 called *Not Just Any Game*, and pass it out to your students. Adjust the last instruction to fit the topic of the lesson chosen for the night. It's a good intro to the topic.
Brad Sorenson

The Return of Leopold

This is a great game to help students to learn one another's names. You need an object. Any object will do, it can be a pocketknife or paper cup—whatever you have on hand. Introduce the object and assign it a name. "This is my key chain, Leopold." Talk about Leopold. Tell how long the two of you have been together. Introduce Leopold to the teen on your left who must introduce him to the next person and so on. The trick is that each person has to say the names of all the people who came before. A typical game goes like this—

(**Youth Leader**): Leopold, my name is Roni, and I'd like to introduce you to Marko.

(See *End of School Blowout* on page 17.)

Find a partner and complete the following instructions—

- Join another couple and discuss your plans for the summer.

- Stop another pair and together sing a few lines of your favorite Beach Boys song.

- Have one of your twosome ride piggyback on the other and high-five three other folks.

- Grab two other couples, sit down, and quickly share (no more than 10 seconds each)—What summer means to me.

- Huddle with three other couples and take turns telling your most and least favorite classes of the year you just finished.

- Play leapfrog with another twosome while all four of you chant, "No more pencils, no more books, no more teachers' dirty looks."

- Sit down with a final pair and make predictions about where you'll all go to college and what you'll major in.

Marko: Hello Leopold. Roni says your name is Leopold. I'm Marko, and I'd like to introduce you to Karla.

Karla: Hello Leopold. Marko said that Roni said your name is Leopold. I'm Karla, and I'd like to introduce you to Mikey.

Mikey: Hello. Karla said that Marko said that Roni said that your name is Leopold. My name is Mikey, and I'd like to introduce you to Dave.

Dave: Hello. Mikey said that Karla said that Marko said that Roni said that your name is Leopold. I'm Dave, and I'd like to introduce you to Nicole.

Nicole: Hello. Dave said that Mikey said that Karla said that Marko said that Roni said that your name is Leopold. My name is Nicole, and I'd like to introduce you to Leoney.

And so on and so on.   *Steve Case*

Amoeba Mixer

Give students each a card with a question on it—such as, What is your favorite color, favorite place to eat, mother's maiden name, or shoe size. Each student answers the question and returns the card without putting her name on it.

Shuffle the cards and distribute them to the students. Students try to find the person described on the card. When the person on the card is found, students join hands and the front person (who has been found but has not yet found his person) takes the other with him to find the person he is looking for. When the last person is found (she is at the end of the line), the line forms a circle. The game is finished, and everyone may sit down. NOTE—Students are not allowed to ask, "Is this your card?"   *Chad Groff*

Ice Breakers

Write two lists and ask the students which they prefer:

Jeans or cargo pants?
Hot or cold?
Staying home or going out?
Loud or quiet?
Burger King or McDonald's?
Pizza or milkshakes?

This will get the group talking and debating. Ask the group, "What is the weirdest thing you've ever eaten?" The group will discover that what some people see as weird, others see as normal. Ask the group to talk about their worst cooking disaster—the first time they tried to cook or tried to impress a date.   *Matt Zarb*

The Exchange Game

Have each student get a partner and form the group into two circles. The inner circle faces out, and the outer circle faces in. When the circles are complete, the partners should be directly facing each other. Now ask each student to exchange some information with each partner, always beginning with the name (for example: name, what school you go to, what grade are you in, what's your favorite flavor of ice cream, etc.). After they have exchanged information have them exchange something from their person (for example: wallet, shoe, necklace, hairclip, etc.). After this first exchange ask the inner circle to move three people to its right. Now everyone has a new partner. Again ask them to exchange some information. Use the same questions as before, or change some or all of them. For example, you may still want them to share what school they go to and what grade they are in, but now you may want them to share what their favorite kind of pizza is. Just make sure they always share their names. Once they've completed sharing their information, ask them to once again exchange something new from their person. It can't be something they already received. It must be something different that belongs to them.

Now ask the outer circle to move three persons to its right, resulting again in a new partner. Have them exchange information and exchange something new from their person. By now everyone should have given away three items.

Now ask the inner circle to move three persons to its right. This time after they exchange information, have each person exchange one of the items received from someone else. Repeat this same process two more times, alternating between the outer and the inner circle, and exchanging items received from other people.

By now everyone should have made six different exchanges, and their stuff will be spread out who knows where. This leads to the final part of the game—Mass Chaos! The final step is to now tell everyone they must get all three of their own items back, and in their proper place. The first one to complete that task can win some kind of a prize or maybe be the first one in line for the food if they're getting ready to eat.

You really need at least about 30 to play this game, but it can be played with groups of more than 100. Obviously you can make many adaptations to this, but making six exchanges—three of your own stuff, and three of someone else's stuff—works best.

Stephen Campbell

Clothespin Relay Mixer

String a clothesline from one end of the room to the other, shoulder high to the average person. Place the clothespins on the line. Teams line up facing the line. The object is to run to the line, remove one clothespin with your teeth (no hands), and bring it back to the team. All team members do the same in relay fashion.

Adrienne Cali

(See *Not Just Any Game* on page 17.)

Not Just any Game

You must have at least 15 *different* names on your page to qualify for the grand prize.

↪ Find four people and sing "Jingle Bells" together

↪ Find two people who can speak three sentences in French

↪ Find another person and carry on the following conversation—

> **You:** Hi, how are you, hello?
>
> **Them:** I'm fine. Do you like Jell-O?
>
> **You:** I do—especially yellow
>
> **Them:** Me too, but not with marshmallow
>
> **You:** How true. Do you play the cello?
>
> **Them:** I do! But only when I feel mellow.

Get signature _____

↪ Stand on a chair; hold your hands in the air, and jump around as if you just don't care (for at least 5 seconds).

Signature of witness _____

↪ Find three people who have eaten at McDonald's within the last week.

↪ Find two other people who have a birthday the same month as you.

↪ Find five other people and form a human pyramid.

↪ Get the signatures of someone from each grade.

Seventh _____

Eighth _____

Ninth _____

Tenth _____

Eleventh _____

Twelfth _____

↪ Find a person who plays each of these sports, and get their signature.

Soccer _____

Hockey _____

Volleyball _____

Football _____

Basketball _____

21

Press Conference

The goal is create a fun, lively forum in which group members not only learn one another's names (by hearing them over and over again), but they also get to find out interesting facts about each other. The whole group simulates an actual press conference. Individuals take turns being interviewed. Group members imitate members of the press corps by raising hands and asking questions. Group leaders can even create a mock podium complete with fake microphones. If the group successfully reproduces the feel of an actual press conference, this exercise will produce a lot of laughs, and help the group become acquainted.

NOTE—If the press corps interviews 12 to 16 people, this exercise will take about an hour by the time you factor in laughing and having people move to and from the podium.

Rules

1. The group (called the press corps) interviews individual group members for 60-90 seconds. Group members may elect to be interviewed with each other or by themselves. The group should appoint someone to act as timekeeper.

2. The press corps may make up its own questions or use the prepared questions on page 23.

3. Before reporters may ask a question, the person(s) being interviewed must be recognized by name.

4. When reporters are called on by name to ask a question, they must stand, repeat their names, and give some sort of identifying description (for example, David McGehee of Bunker Hill High or Jo Peterson of Danbury). Then they may address a question to the interviewee(s).

5. Interviewees should answer quickly and keep their answers brief so at least five to six questions can be asked. Long pauses while people ponder how to respond will result in a long, boring press conference.

6. Continue until everyone is interviewed.

7. When the allotted interview time runs out, the person being interviewed can make a brief closing remark. They then rejoin the press corps, and the press corps interviews someone else or another couple.

Len Woods

(See *Press Conference* on page 22.)

Press Conference

Sample Questions for the Press Corps:

- How tall are you?
- How do you fill your days?
- What is your favorite hobby?
- How do you feel at this very moment?
- How should we interpret your hesitation to answer that last question?
- Who in this youth group have you known the longest?
- Trick Question—When did you stop shoplifting?
- Where were you raised?
- Tell us your brothers or sisters if you have any.
- What were your first impressions of your boyfriend/girlfriend?
- What were your first impressions of _____ Church?
- What desserts or foods would you like to consume at these meetings?
- What is your favorite Bible story or passage?
- What is the best movie you've seen in the last 6 months?
- What is the best book you've read in the last 6 months?
- If you could have any car, what model would you choose and why?
- If you were entering college today, what major would you choose and why?

- What section of the newspaper do you read first and why?
- What are your best and worst habits?
- What city would you like to visit?
- What Olympic event do you most enjoy watching and why?
- What magazines do you read on a regular basis?
- Name one of your pet peeves.
- Finish this statement: My family _____.
- Finish this statement: My world consists of mainly _____.
- If you had a free day with no responsibilities, no obligations, and no schedule, how would you spend it?
- How could the worship services at your church be improved?
- Why did you choose to get involved in this particular group?
- When in your life did you feel closest to God?
- What should the United States do about the situation in _____?
- What in a nutshell do you think about the President?
- What is in your favorite meal?
- Some people think our group should go on a mission trip together. Where would you like to see this group go and why?

23

(See *Beach-O-Rama* on page 25.)

Beach-O-Rama

As quickly and accurately as possible, work your way through the following list:

1. Find a fair-skinned person and ask, "Wow! How'd you get such a great tan?" Get a signature here. _____

2. Get with three other people. Two of you circle the other two, humming the theme song from the movie *Jaws*, while the other two scream for 10 seconds. Have one person initial here. _____

3. Walk around the room with your hands out like you're surfing, and say to five different people, "I can out-surf you and your whole family any day of the week!" The fifth person signs here. _____

4. Ask three different people to be your Beach Baby. The third signs here.

   _____

5. Go up to someone you barely know and give him or her a 10-second speech on why the ocean tastes salty. Get a signature here.

   _____

6. Jump up and down 10 times waving your arms, and then yell, "Everybody out of the water!" Get a witness to sign here.

   _____

7. Tell someone the riddle below, and then fall on the floor and laugh hysterically for five full seconds.
   Q: Do you know why you can never get hungry at the beach?
   A: Because of the sand which is (sandwiches) there!
       That person initials here. _____

8. Ask someone what the weather forecast is for tomorrow and then giggle uncontrollably. He or she should sign here. _____

9. Get with two other people, lie on the floor, and pretend to swim while singing—"This is the way we swim to Hawaii, swim to Hawaii, swim to Hawaii. This is the way we swim to Hawaii, so early in the morning." Get one of your partners to initial here.

   _____

Pipeline Mixer

Have students divide into teams of 8 to 20. Give everyone a straw, have them line up, and get on their knees. Each team chooses a sipper (you may even give them a sipper hat) who goes to the far end of the line. At the signal, they must join their straws together and form a pipeline so the sipper can sip a Coke from a cup.

Adrienne Cali

Dog Biscuit Relay Mixer

This hilarious relay works great for any size group. If your group is large, divide into teams of five or more players. If your group is small, divide into two teams and repeat the relay two or more times to determine the winning team. Have each team form a straight line with each team member down on all fours (like a dog) facing forward. Give group members each a pinch-type clothespin to put in their mouth so the clothespin can be opened and closed with their teeth. Put a bowl with 10 or 12 dog biscuits on the floor in front of each team's line. The first person in each team's line must take the dog biscuits out of the bowl one at a time, using the clothespin in his mouth. He then passes the biscuit to the next person and so on down the line. If someone drops a biscuit, the person who dropped it must pick it up with the clothespin. No hands are allowed at any time. Teams must stay in a straight line and remain on hands and knees throughout the relay. The first team to put all its biscuits in the bowl at the end of the line wins.

Adrienne Cali

Beach-O-Rama

This mixer combines crazy activities and opportunities to get acquainted. It works best in groups of 20 and up and is great during the summer or during trips to beach areas. Play this as a competition, and give out a prize or simply set a time limit. Give each person a copy of the handout on page 24.

Len Woods

Penny Crowd Breaker

Everyone gets 10 pennies. A large bowl is put in the middle of the circle and each person has a turn. When each turn comes, that person tells the group one thing they've never done. Anyone in the group who *has* done what the person said throws a penny in the bowl. Some examples are—I've never flown in a plane or I've never been out of the United States. The last person holding a penny wins.

Rick McCall

Never Have I Ever

[Variation on Penny Crowd Breaker]

Have everyone sit in a circle of chairs with one person in the middle. Make sure there are no empty chairs in the circle. The person in the middle says, "Hi, I'm..." The group responds, "Hi..." The person then says, "Never have I ever..." and indicates something he has never done (for example, been to France, sung in a choir, eaten sushi).

Everyone who has done whatever is named must stand and move to a different chair. A person can never return to the chair she just left. While everyone moves, the person in the middle tries to sit in a vacant chair. The person left standing is the new person in the middle.

Don Mullins

Hollingsworth

Have a group (no more than 12) sit train-style in chairs. Students face the back of the person in front of them. The object of the game is to get to and stay in the number one chair.

The person sitting in chair number one begins. He calls out his own number in a loud voice followed by another person's number. If "One Six!" were called out, number six would then call out his own number and someone else's: "Six Four!" Number four does the same thing. If someone messes up or says "Um...Ur...or Ahhh" the youth leader sounds a buzzer or bell and that person moves to the last chair. Everyone else moves up one chair and takes on a new number. Number one starts again.

This is a deceptively simple game. The quicker it moves, the more fun it is. Your job as the youth leader is to gradually increase to lightning speed. The youth leader may play the game but must also be the judge. Start them off slowly, but eventually you must be heartless with the buzzer.

Steve Case

Oh, Sit!

This is a silly little get-to-know-you game. Pass out paper and pencils. Have students write short biographies about themselves or write about a bizarre event that happened to them the previous week. Then have students trade papers.

Tell them to imagine that these papers were written on a very old typewriter that had a broken letter *H*. Next, have each player go through the sheet and cross out or remove all of the *H*s. Then have the students read the biography aloud as it's now written.

Steve Case

Marbles

You'll need Styrofoam cups and marbles.

Before handing out the cups, make a marble-sized hole somewhere in the bottom of each cup. The hole could also be in the side near the bottom. Vary the location of the hole in each cup.

Form two lines (maybe guys versus girls) and hand out the cups. Students hold the cups in their mouths.

Explain that you'll drop a marble into the first student's cup. The student then must roll the marble around in the cup until it drops through the marble-sized hole into the next student's cup. If the marble misses the cup, put it back in the previous cup. Watching students writhe around to get the marble into the next cup is hilarious. Have each line do five marbles. *Paul Turner*

Meeting Opener Games

The ideas Library

FOR YOUTH GROUPS

Turn Around

Rather everyone in a circle facing away from the center. If the group is too large for the room, form more than one circle. Have everyone hold hands, and then give them this challenge. Work together to turn the circle around so that everyone is facing the center. The problem is you can't let go of each other's hands. It can be done! Everyone has to work together.

This game helps define the students who are natural leaders as well as those who facilitate or follow well. The more people involved the better.

It's a good crowd breaker and point maker. People are forced to touch each other when they hold hands and duck in and out between each other. People have to talk with each other to make suggestions, which helps in learning names and developing leadership. And people share the reward of working together and achieving what at first seems to be impossible. *Dave Milliken*

Test of Strength

Ask two female volunteers to lie on a collapsed table with their feet hanging over one end. Then get some strong guys to gradually lift up one end of table. The two contestants try to hang on with their feet. Whoever stays on the longest wins. Then get two guys to do the same thing. *Robyn Bridgeo*

Questions Only

Get two teams of volunteers in front of the room and ask the audience for topics. Choose a topic and have the first person on each team shout a question to the first person on the other team. If one person takes too long (five seconds or more), or if he says something that is not in the form of a question, send him to the end of his team's line. Continue until you want quiet. *Souled Out Youth Ministries*

A sample game topic

Shopping for Underwear

Team 1: Does this make me look fat?

Team 2: Why are you asking me?

Team 1: Didn't I come here with you?

Team 2: What?

Group Building

Make an abstract object from *Lego* or *Duplo* bricks. Don't let anyone see this object.

Break your group into smaller groups of equal size. Have each small group choose a leader. Leaders go to the front of the room where the hidden object is. They can have a predetermined time to inspect it without touching or moving the object. They then go back to their groups where they try to tell the group how to build the object. The group must build the object. The leader, who knows what they are building, may only talk to her small group.

VARIATION—Sometime during the building session, project a slide of the object from different angles on the screen or have another member come up and look at the object so two people can communicate to the group.

NOTE—Make sure you have enough of each of the pieces for the original creation to be duplicated by each group.

Beth Duron

Winter Wackiness

This mixer combines crazy activity and opportunities for students to get acquainted. It works best in groups of 20 or more during winter ski trips, in hilly retreat settings, or during the holidays. Give each person a copy of the handout on page 33, and play as a competition with a prize, or simply set a time limit.

Len Woods

I Game

Make copies of one side of a dollar bill or buy some cheap play money. Give everyone in the group four of the fake bucks, then just mingle and talk to people. Anyone who says *I*, as in referring to self, must give up one dollar to the person who caught him. Give only one buck to the first person who catches it, and if no one catches it, you keep the money. Some players will go broke quickly, some will get rich, and some will learn to trick people into saying *I*. Students realize how much they refer to themselves, and it's a great opener for discussions about being self-centered.

Victor Holland

Movie Match

You'll need a tape player, a tape with various sound bites on it (see below), and something like a chalkboard or whiteboard to keep score on.

Gather sound bites from a couple dozen movies (or TV shows, if you want to use those instead), some well-known and some more obscure. Use discretion about the movies you choose to use. Divide the students into two or more teams. You could do guys-against-girls if that works for your group.

Play the clips and have students shout out the correct answers. The team which identifies the clip first wins a point. If you think some of the movies are more difficult, make them worth more points.

Brian Stegner

(See *Winter Wackiness* on page 32.)

Winter Wackiness

As quickly and accurately as possible, work your way through the following list:

1. Get with three other people. Imitate champion ice skaters, and slide your way around the room twice.

    Get one of your partners to initial here _____

2. Grab someone and together sing two lines of any song you can think of with the word *snow* in it. Get that person to put his or her John Hancock right here _____

3. Join hands with someone else and run around the room for 10 seconds as if you were catching snowflakes on your tongues.

    Your partner initials here _____

4. Jump up on a chair, look out the window, get a frightened look on your face, and shout, "Avalanche!"

    Get a witness to sign here _____

5. Wish five people, "Season's Greetings!"

    The fifth person initials here _____

6. Pull someone aside and together pretend to be suffering from hypothermia. Shivering, shaking, and with chattering teeth, find someone older and whine, "It's cold in here! Turn on the heat!"

    That person signs here _____

7. Find three other people and together pretend to bobsled your way around the entire room.

    One of them signs here _____

8. Do your best fake sneeze. Find the person who initialed number 3 above and have him rate you here on a scale of 1 to10 (1 is fake beyond words and 10 is so real I thought I had snot on me)

    Signature _____

Uhhh!

Give students a topic and 30 seconds to name 7 items in that topic without saying *uhhh*, *ummm*, *ahhh*, or any other pausing phrase. You can make up your own topics, but some suggestions are things that are red, things that are blue, things you turn off (or on), things that fly, pro or college mascots, books of the Bible, disciples, things you ride.

Give them the topic, and start the time immediately. Don't give them any time to think about it.
Monty Eastman

Hoppity-Hop Jousting

Start with two parallel lines, two players, and two Hoppity Hop balls—you know, those big round bouncy balls with handles that you played with as a kid.

Give each contestant a pie tin filled with whipped cream. Students bounce their way along the line and throw their pie tins at the opposing players as in real old-time medieval jousts.

Award different points, depending on where they land a hit. (For example, give 10 points for the head, five points for the torso, and three points for the limbs.) *Jason Djang*

Hollywood Squares

You need nine chairs up front, small whiteboards (or nine large papers printed with an *O* and nine large papers printed with an *X*), nine witty counselors or volunteers (this works best with counselors), and a list of questions (probably 15 or so for one round to be played).

Place the nine chairs in three rows (so they resemble a tick-tack-toe square), place one counselor in each chair (these counselors can have celebrity identities for an added twist), and get two contestants from the audience.

The host has a list of questions that can be Bible trivia, random questions about your church or whatever you choose as a focus. The two contestants (one is *X*, and one is *O*) take turns choosing a counselor to answer the host's next question. As the counselor answers, the contestant decides if she agrees or disagrees with the answer given. If she's correct, she get the square. Witty, sarcastic comments are always welcome from the counselors when they are called upon.

Melissa Dickinson

Ahh! Game

Get everyone in a circle (this works best with a maximum of about 15 students per circle). One person starts by pointing with both hands and arms to someone else while screaming, "Ahh!" Whoever is pointed at raises his arms and points to the sky screaming, "Ahh!" The two people on either side of him simultaneously point to him with both arms and hands and scream, "Ahh!" The first person then points at another person in the circle while—you guessed it—screaming, "Ahh!" And it all repeats. It's a rhythm game, so therefore when someone breaks the rhythm, he's out. Play until you get two winners. *Jason Djang*

Snot Rag Shot Put

You need tissue paper, duct tape, and a measuring tape for this game. Each team makes a shot put out of tissue paper and a small piece of duct tape. The smaller the duct tape the more creative the students have to be.

Then each team tosses its shot put. Measure the distance of the tosses with the measuring tape. The team that throws its shot put farthest wins. *Jeff Mattesich*

Alarm Clocks Are Evil

Divide your group into teams, and play the game as a relay. You need one digital alarm clock for each team. The first person in line races across the room and sets the alarm clock for one minute past its current setting. Then she must race across the room to a pillow and blanket. The player must lie down with head on the pillow, cover up with the blanket, and snore loudly three times. When the alarm sounds, she races to turn it off before running back and tagging the next player. If the alarm goes off before the player lies down, covers up, and snores three times, the contestant must start over. *Jeff Mattesich*

The Window

This game is based on the following song;

"The window, the window, the second story window,

With a heave and a ho and a mighty throw,
They threw it out the window."

Break the group into two groups—guys against girls always works well. If the group is large, give each group a microphone. The leader (with a guitar or band) sings the cheesy song as the chorus throughout the entire game. Everyone will catch on quickly, so you don't have to teach the song right away. As the verse to the song, a member from each team must sing a nursery rhyme in the rhythm of the chorus and add the line "and threw it out the window" instead of the final line. For instance, "Jack and Jill went up the hill to fetch a pail of water, Jack fell down and broke his crown, and threw it out the window," then together the team sings the chorus. The competition ends when one team's member either repeats a rhyme or can't think of a new one. The leader can decide on the amount of grace time to give a team to begin singing its verse. *David Rydman*

Crisco Kid

You need a table, two chairs, and some Crisco. This is an old-fashioned arm-wrestling match with the added twist of greasing students' arms and hands in Crisco. It's messy, but it works best if the students have a lot of Crisco on their arms. Just watch this one as students flop around and the old game of strength becomes a game of skill and mostly luck. Have paper towels nearby for cleanup. *Jeff Mattesich*

Shop Vac Suck

You need two shop vacuums, pinto beans, pennies, marbles, and blindfolds. Ahead of time set up a course full of the beans, pennies, and marbles.

Blindfold two student volunteers. As the blindfolded students travel around trying to suck up the items, have the rest of the youth group yell directions to where the items are. Assign point values to each item, and select two teams of three to count the points. The person with the most points wins.

This is a noisy game because the vacuums make lots of noise, the stuff being sucked up makes noise, and the students all yell. *Jeff Mattesich*

Scope Off

You need a bottle of Scope mouthwash and cups. Have students put Scope in their mouths and swish it around until the "sting" makes them spit. Last one with the Scope in her mouth wins.

For a variation have different flavors of mouthwash hidden underneath a towel on a table and have each contestant choose the one they will gargle without knowing the flavor. *Jeff Mattesich*

play this as a battle-of-the-sexes game). Place a cracker on the table and have players go back and forth saying, "I'll eat that cracker with sardines," for example. With each turn, the players add another condiment to the cracker. When a player backs out and says, "Eat that cracker!" the other player must eat the cracker with all of the condiments on it. Have a really good prize, not a gag prize, for the winner. (Get it? GAG prize?)   *Kevin Terry*

Breakfast of Champions

Take a five-gallon bucket and fill it with one pound of flour, one gallon of sugar syrup, a large can of Quaker Oats, and two quarts of orange juice (nice little breakfast combo). Put 15 to 20 small objects such as dice or marbles in the bucket and stir. Give each contestant a plastic spoon, and when you say "Go", they try to fish out as many of the objects, as they can in two minutes. Put plastic sheeting under the buckets, because this game gets messy! Students will most likely ditch the spoon in favor of just pawing through the goo.   *Alex Roller*

Easter Peep Rescue

Oh no! Easter Peeps have been trapped in the mud pit and must be rescued! Fill a shallow aluminum baking pan with chocolate sauce. Stick Easter Peeps (puffy marshmallow candy bunnies or chicks) in the mud pit with some totally submerged and others partially sticking out. Students must then race to rescue the Peeps from utter peril! Rescue methods could vary. Students can only use their mouths, scoop them out with a spoon or fork held between their toes, or use a spoon or fork held in their teeth—whatever you come up with! *Alex Roller*

Gummy Games

Give your students a package of gummy worms, and let them race to spell the words you give them—using their gummy worms. To make the game more interesting, allow them to move their gummy worms into place using only their tongues.

Use gummy worms, bears, fish, cherries, etc. to play a big game of Pictionary. Use the standard rules of no words, letters, or numbers, and use gummies instead of markers. This game can be played on the floor on butcher paper, or use a dry erase board or Plexi-glass and have students stick the gummies to the board.

VARIATION—Using a homemade paper target, a child's dartboard, or a hunting target, have students lick and flick gummy bears at the target. Make each concentric circle worth more points as they move toward the center. Form teams of students by grades, and play the game as a relay—one person gets one to stick, then tags the next team member. *Alex Roller*

Plunger Sundaes

This game grosses teens out, and it's a lot of fun. You need two new toilet plungers and the fixin's for ice cream sundaes. You can get the new plungers fairly cheap at a hardware store. Make ice cream sundaes with chocolate syrup inside the plungers.

Ask for pairs of volunteers (it's more fun if they don't know what they're volunteering for). One person holds the new plunger while the other person eats the sundae with a spoon. (NOTE—You can play this so the eaters have to keep their hands behind their backs. Videotape this one for added fun.) The first pair to finish the entire sundae wins. What do they win? You guessed it—a plunger! *Andy Merritt*

Gone Fishin'

Outside or on a floor that can be mopped, circle everyone up or choose teams for a relay. Have students close their eyes (or blindfold them) and pass a stuffed animal (preferably a fish) around the circle. Everyone must handle the item. Use a timer to spice up the competition. Do this a number of times for dramatic effect. Catch or purchase ahead of time several large fish from a local fish market, grocery meat department or grocery store. With their eyes still closed (the students' eyes, that is!), introduce the real fish into the relay. The reactions will be hysterical. Continue with the race until everyone has participated at least once. *David Vaughn*

Pop-Tart Memories

Purchase a box of every flavor of Pop-Tarts from your local supermarket. Cut them up and then blindfold students. See if students can guess the correct flavor by taste alone.

Afterward have a discussion about favorite breakfast cereals or Pop-Tarts. Ask students what kind of flavor they would create if they worked for Kellogg's. Serve warm Pop-Tarts with ice cream as a snack. *Steve Case*

Cracker Castles

Divide your group into teams and give each team a few boxes of various shaped crackers. Using a jar of Cheez Whiz as mortar, tell them to create a castle made entirely out of crackers. Give prizes to the most creative, tallest, or most bizarre. When they finish, let them eat one another's castles.   *Steve Case*

Squirrels

You need several big bags of walnuts in the shell. Prior to the game go through the bag, and write a number on each nut (label them 1 to 200, or assign each one five points with a few 10 pointers thrown in for bonuses). The more nuts you have, the better. Hide these all over your church building. Make them obvious enough so students don't have to dig through wastebaskets or open the pastor's drawers.

Divide your group into teams and say, "Go!" The team that gets the most points wins. One team can have more nuts, but if the other team has higher point values, they can still win.

VARIATION—Tie the teams together by the wrists so they stay together at all times. If a team comes back with the string broken and retied, they lose points. *Steve Case*

Candied Onion

Create a competition to eat a candied apple, except make one of the apples a candied onion. Keep track of the onion, and be sure it goes to a person who won't be too embarrassed when they discover the trick.   *Brett Durham*

I Want Candy

Bring in a bag of every sort of candy you can get your hands on (the more the better). Have students sit in a circle and take turns choosing one candy bar and using it to describe something about themselves. For example, "I'm the best basketball player on my team BAR-NONE." "I like getting KISSES from my boyfriend." "I have a KIT-KAT at home named Fluffy." Praise students who are extra creative. When the game is over, cut all the bars up into small pieces, and let everyone share in them all.   *Steve Case*

Incredible Edible Challenges

These fun icebreakers all involve food, and are variations on other mixers. Consider making these all part of a pentathlon event!

Jalapeno Contest. Ask several students to participate in the contest, and then unveil the jalapeno and banana peppers. Students must put them in their mouths, chew three times without swallowing, and see who can hold the pepper in her mouth the longest.

Spelling Bee. Have a bowl of Alpha-Bits cereal for each student, and have students race to spell various words using only their tongues and their bowls of cereal. Use words related to your lesson topic, random words, or the name of your ministry!

NOTE—Make sure that the letters exist for the words you ask the students to spell.

Go Fish. Give each student a pie tin full of whipped cream with gummy worms buried in the whipped cream. Students can use only their mouths to fish out as many gummy worms as possible in the allotted time (about 30 to 60 seconds).

NOTE—Cool Whip works better, but if you use whipped cream, put it in the tins immediately before the game—it turns to liquid in a short time.

M&M Sort. Give each student a bowl of M&M's. Using only their mouths, students must separate out the brown M&M's and put them in a cup. At the end of 60 to 90 seconds, give students two points for each brown M&M in the cup, and subtract one point for each colored M&M in the cup.

Farley's Fruit Snack Challenge. In this game, two-people teams compete to see who can get the most Farley's Fruit Snacks to stick to their partner's face in 60 seconds. Have as many teams as you want—use leaders, or use the entire group!

Alex Roller

Musical Belches

Have your group sit in a circle, and give each student (except one) a paper cup of water. One student gets a cup of soda pop. Play some music and have the students pass their cups around the circle. When the music stops, whoever is holding the soda cup must drink it as fast as possible. Refill the soda cup, and continue to play.

Steve Case

Taste Test Mixer

Fill small cups with similar colored soda (Dr. Pepper, Coke, Vanilla Coke, etc.), and assign each soda by name to different teams. Tell the entire group that they have to try to find the members of their team. Obviously, the only way to do that is to taste one another's drinks. By the end of this game, the group will be full of caffeine, unless you plan accordingly!

NOTE—Keep an eye on the group before you begin to see if anyone has the sniffles. If someone seems sick, bag this game in favor of another one. *Mike Arldt*

Whipped Cream M&M's

You'll need one bag of M&M's, eight large cans of whipped cream, four large bowls, a tarp to protect the floor, one table, and lots of paper towels.

Fill the bowls with the whipped cream shortly before you begin. Otherwise it will liquefy. As you fill the bowls with whipped cream, drop 30 M&M's in each bowl. Set up a table and place the tarp underneath to protect the carpet or floor.

Ask for two boys and two girls to volunteer to play. Bring out the bowls and set them on the table. Tell the students the object of the game is to eat all 30 M&Ms in the whipped cream without using their hands. They'll have to prove they've picked up an M&M—by showing it on the tongue to the group—before consuming each!

George Husk

WORD GAMES AND QUIZZES

THE *ideas* LIBRARY

And in Local News—a TV Quiz

You need a local listing of television stations, what channels they are on, a hat full of TV station numbers, and two bells. Divide your group in half according to where they are sitting. Choose a number from the hat. The first student to run up and ring in with the name of the television or cable network, or station call-letters, gets the point. The first team to get 10 points wins (This game is a great setup for a media-influence night.) A variation of this game is to have students say the name of a show and what time it is on the given station. *Jeff Mattesich*

Game Shows

Use game show formats, and alter the questions and answers. Use the game show theme for a couple of months, and start every youth group with a different game show. For example, *Jeopardy*, *Wheel of Fortune*, *Joker's Wild*, *$10,000 Pyramid*, *Street Smarts*, and *Do You Want to Be a Millionaire?* are easy to adapt. Use Microsoft's PowerPoint to make the games look snazzy.

For *Jeopardy* make a large board and stick the questions to the board. Then either cover them up or flip them over when someone chooses that category and numerical value. Be creative in your category selection. Use Biblical themes, review recent lessons, ask random staff trivia, or make announcements—the possibilities are endless.

Wheel of Fortune is great for announcing upcoming events. Just make the announcement the phrase students try to guess.

Street Smarts is fun if you actually catch people off guard when you ask them questions. Wake students up early with a video camera interview. Or film people walking out of church who don't expect to be interviewed. Dropping video clips into media presentation is easier in Media Shout than PowerPoint. *Jenny Mattesich*

Cereal Scriptures

Have your students form teams of two or three people. Give each team a pile of Alpha-Bits cereal. Have them read the Scripture verses below, think of a one- or two-word phrase to summarize the entire verse, and use their cereal letters to spell it out. For an added challenge have the group spell the world BIBLE between them. Then all other words must begin or end with one of the letters in BIBLE. *Scott Meier*

Psalm 23:1-2	Ephesians 5:2	Colossians 4:5
Psalm 23:3-4	Ephesians 6:1I	Timothy 6:6-10
Matthew 28:18-20	Philippians 3:7-9I	Timothy 6:12
Ephesians 2:8-9	Philippians 3:10-11I	John 1:5
Ephesians 2:10	Colossians 4:2I	John 1:8-9

Youth Worker's Quiz

Gather information from your youth leaders using the forms on page 67:

Use the answers to make a quiz. Read the facts aloud, and have your students guess which youth leader you're talking about (It's also fun to make up a few out-there facts to see which leader the students match with the made-up fact).

Tom Daniel

Guess the Leader

You need two pictures of your youth leaders when they were in junior high, and two bells. The pictures can be placed in a PowerPoint or MediaShout presentation. Divide your group into two teams, show the first image, and ask the students to identify the person in the picture. If students know the answer, they run up to the front and ring the bell. The first one to ring in with the correct answer gets the point. The team with the most points wins.

A variation of this game is to use photos of leaders, pastors, or students. When you put them into your presentation, show a small section of the picture that has been enlarged. Then on each following slide, pull out farther and farther from the close-up. For example, if in the first slide the screen is filled with just an image of an eye, show the eye, nose, and cheek in the next slide. In the third slide show the whole face, and in the fourth slide show the face and the hair. By the fifth slide show the whole picture. When a student rings in, stop the slide progression. *Jeff Mattesich*

Quick Questions

This fast get-to-know-you game can be played as one group or in teams. Choose

Youth Worker's Quiz

(See *Youth Worker's Quiz* on page 66.)

➲ Name _____

➲ Birthplace and hometown _____

➲ Hobbies and talents (for example, any unusual collections or special abilities) _____

_____

➲ Junior high and high school awards or honors (for example, Mr. or Mrs. High School, most likely to succeed, or drum major) _____

_____

➲ Funny or embarrassing moments in junior high and high school (for example, five speeding tickets in 11th grade, or blew up chemistry lab) _____

_____

➲ Other interesting information about you (for example, Chippendale dancer in college, or went to school with or is related to famous person) _____ (write on back)

Youth Worker's Quiz

➲ Name _____

➲ Birthplace and hometown _____

➲ Hobbies and talents (for example, any unusual collections or special abilities) _____

_____

➲ Junior high and high school awards or honors (for example, Mr. or Mrs. High School, most likely to succeed, or drum major) _____

_____

➲ Funny or embarrassing moments in junior high and high school (for example, five speeding tickets in 11th grade, or blew up chemistry lab) _____

_____

➲ Other interesting information about you (for example, Chippendale dancer in college, or went to school with or is related to famous person) _____ (write on back)

a leader for each group to be the keeper of the questions. Have each team form a circle. Each member of the group must answer each question one at a time. The leader asks the questions. The group must answer all of the questions or perform the assigned tasks. The team that completes the entire list first wins. If you play with one group, start a timer and see how quickly they can get through the list.

Ken Lane

1. Everyone's name
2. Everyone's favorite hobby
3. The city or township that everyone lives in
4. What each person wants to be in life
5. Everyone's favorite TV show
6. Everyone's favorite fast food restaurant
7. Everyone's shoe size
8. The year each person graduates
9. Number of people in the group who drive
10. Number of people in the group wearing Nike shoes
11. Number of girls in the group
12. Total number of pieces of clothing being worn by your group
13. Shake hands with everyone in your group
14. Have everyone stand on the left foot
15. Number of people who like Mickey Mouse
16. Have everyone touch everyone else's knee
17. Have all members sign the paper with their first and last names

Best Friends

You'll need eight volunteers (two teams of four) and a list of prepared questions. Place two chairs facing the audience. Place two long tables behind the chairs. Meet with one person from each group a few minutes before you play the game. Ask a series of questions about their group of friends, such as "Of the four of you, who is most likely to watch the most TV?" or "Who of you is most likely to get the best grade in math?" Write down all of the answers. Make sure the two people you speak with have no contact with their other friends before the game begins.

The two people who answered the questions sit in the chairs up front. The three others on each team stand behind the tables and answer the questions. Ask the questions alternating between teams. If the team's answer matches its representative's answer, it wins five points. The two sitting up front can't look back or make any movements; they can only give their answer after their friends have answered. If the answers don't match, the team loses five points. It's anyone's game up until the very end.

Melissa Dickinson

Sample Questions
Which of you has the messiest room at home?
Which of you is most likely to get the best grade in math?
Which of you would find the best bargain while shopping?
Which of you would score higher on _____ (a video game or sports)?
Which of you is most likely to end up in detention?
Which of you would be more likely to talk their way out of detention?

Which of you knows would do best on Bible Jeopardy?
Which of you guys is most likely to become famous?
Which of you spends the most time on the Internet?
Which of you could survive longest on a deserted island?
Which of you would be the first to try to drink a gallon of milk in one hour?
Which of you has the cutest clothes?

Stax O' Fax

Give each student a slip of paper with an interesting and amusing fact. At the signal students should try to share their facts with as many other people as possible. After several minutes have the students sit down and take a quiz with questions about all of the same facts. Award a prize to the person who gets the most right.

Len Cuthbert

Sample Facts

A duck's quack does not echo.

In the 1940s the FCC assigned television's Channel 1 to mobile services (2-way radios in taxicabs, for instance) but did not renumber the other channel assignments. That is why your TV set has channels 2 and up, but no channel 1.

The "save" icon on Microsoft Works shows a floppy disk with the shutter on backwards.

The letter combination *ough* can be pronounced in nine different ways. The following sentence contains them all: "A rough-coated, dough-faced, thoughtful ploughman strode through the streets of Scarborough; after falling into a slough, he coughed and hiccoughed."

The verb *cleave* may be the only English word with two synonyms that are antonyms of each other: 'adhere' and 'separate.'

The only 15-letter word that can be spelled without repeating a letter is *uncopyrightable*.

Facetious and *abstemious* contain all the vowels in alphabetical order, as does *arsenious*, which means 'containing arsenic.'

Emus and kangaroos cannot walk backwards, and both are on the Australian coat of arms for that reason.

Cats have more than 100 vocal sounds while dogs have only about 10.

The word *checkmate* in chess comes from the Persian phrase *Shah Mat*, which means 'the king is left behind.'

Pinocchio is Italian for *pine head*.

Camel's milk does not curdle.

In every episode of *Seinfeld* a Superman figure appears somewhere.

An animal epidemic is called an epizootic.

Murphy's Oil Soap is the chemical most commonly used to clean elephants.

The United States has never lost a war in which mules were used.

Blueberry Jelly Bellys were created especially for Ronald Reagan.

All porcupines float in water.

"Hang on, Sloopy" is the official rock song of Ohio.

Pez comes in coffee flavor.

Lorne Greene had one of his nipples bitten off by an alligator while he was host of *Lorne Greene's Wild Kingdom*.

I Know Spiderman

Take a page from a popular comic book and Wite-Out the words in the dialog balloons. Make copies and pass them out to your students along with some fine-pointed markers or really sharp pencils. Have the students write a creative dialog between the hero and the villain in which they discuss the person who is doing the writing. Hang these up on your youth room wall.

VARIATION—Use different pages for each student, and then fasten them together. Make sure every student gets a copy of *Spiderman Meets the Youth Group*!

Steve Case

STUNTS AND WIDE GAMES

THE *ideas* LIBRARY

FOR YOUTH GROUPS

Invisible Obstacle Course

This game is a practical joke. Choose students with good self-esteem who will not get embarrassed easily. Set up a basic obstacle course with a few obstacles to go around, under, or over. Take three or four volunteers through it, and make sure they are familiar with the course. Then instruct them that they have to go through the course blindfolded, with you guiding them through it verbally (even the audience can help). After they are blindfolded, secretly remove the obstacles so nothing is left but an empty room. The results are hilarious as the contestants try to maneuver their way around an empty room. *Jason Andrews*

Pool Jousting

You need a pool and inner tubes for this great summertime pool game. Have students sit inside inner tubes, with their bottoms in the holes, and move around the pool using their arms. The goal is to be the last one sitting in your inner tube as everyone tries to flip each other over. Stop and do rounds if everyone gets too far away from each other.

Jeff Mattesich

Bunko Mania

Divide into groups of six. Distribute three dice to each group. Play begins after everyone in the group is introduced. The youngest person in each group starts. Each person must keep track of his/her own score just as in regular Bunko. Every #1 rolled in Round One scores a point. A Bunko (all three dice showing the number corresponding to the round) wins the round and stops all play for every team. So if a contestant gets a Bunko, he must jump up and scream, "BUNKO!" If a player rolls and all three dice match the number of the preceding round, the roller is assessed a *You're too late* penalty of five points. If all three of the dice match the number of the next round, the roller is assessed a *You're too early* penalty of five points.

When a Bunko is called, one person in each group immediately takes the three dice, holds them over his head, and forms another group of six with different people. Following introductions, play continues through six rounds. If players tie in number of total wins, those players play a final game up front with the audience cheering an assigned favorite.

Prizes are awarded for most wins and most Bunkos. In just a few short minutes each student can meet and interact with 36 different people. *Kevin Turner*

Stuck on You

You need two coveralls, lots of Velcro (adhesive is best), a hot glue gun, two volunteers, lots of ping-pong balls, and two pairs of goggles.

Have someone cover the coveralls with the rough hooked side of the Velcro by hot gluing it to the suit (be thorough; it looks funnier). Have someone else cover the ping-pong balls with pieces of the soft looped side of the Velcro.

Divide the group into two teams, and have one volunteer from each team put on the coveralls and goggles. Distribute the ping-pong balls to the rest of the students. While they are seated, they try to cover their teammates with ping-pong balls. The team with the most coverage wins. This game works best with white Velcro and black lights (in a dark room). For a more active game, set the two volunteers loose in the church as fugitives, and release the students to try to capture them by covering the other team's volunteer with colored ping-pong balls.

Melissa Dickinson

Sumo Bouncers

You need eight inner tubes for car tires and two bicycle helmets.

Mark the outline of a wrestling ring with tape on the ground and designate four people to be corner posts. Contestants place three or four (depending on the height) inner tubes around their torsos with their arms on the inside. Place a helmet on each player. The idea is to bounce the other player out of the ring or knock them off their feet. The best of three hits is the winner.

SAFETY NOTE—Make sure contestants are about the same size, play on a soft surface, and have plenty of room on the outside of the ring to fall down. *GC, Australia*

Video Quiz

Go to students' houses early in the morning (after checking with parents, of course) and wake them up on video. Ask them a trivia question or ask them do something physical such as using Hula Hoop or eating a banana.

That week at the youth group meeting use the video for your game. Show the video as the question or challenge is asked, and pause it before the student answers. Have students guess if the student will answer correctly—or perform the challenge. Award points accordingly.

Jenny Mattesich

Buckin' Bronco

For this game you need a large plastic or wooden barrel (plastic is easier since it's lightweight), many feet of climbing rope, a saddle, some old cowboy clothes, and a few old mattresses.

Drill a hole on the top and bottom of the barrel and string the rope through it. Then secure the rope to a rafter, or a secure bolt in the ceiling or high on the wall on either side of the room. You could also construct a frame to hold the ropes so nothing attaches to the walls. Place the saddle on the barrel and bolt it to the barrel through the straps underneath to secure it well. Place mattresses under the barrel where the students might fall.

Get a willing contestant who is brave and nimble. Place a hat and cowboy boots on her and saddle up! (Getting on is half the challenge!) Have a counselor on each side to shake the ropes. As the contestants fall off, keep time to see who can stay on the longest.

Melissa Dickinson

I Can Fly

Find someone in your church with rock-climbing knowledge, and find a place to hang two students from the ceiling in climbing harnesses. Give each contestant a helmet and fishing nets. Have students on the ground throw balls up to the suspended students so they can catch them in their nets. Once they catch a ball, they have to drop it from their nets into a bucket below. The climber with most balls in the bucket at the end of the time period wins. This could be a class versus class game or a guys versus girls game.

Jenny Mattesich

Wonder Woman

Form teams of six players and designate one to be Wonder Woman. Make duct-tape bracelets for Wonder Woman with the sticky side facing out. Then have her five teammates stand a certain distance away. The teammates make slingshots using a rubber band strung between their thumb and pointer finger. Using their rubber band slingshots and mini marshmallows, the goal is to see which Wonder Woman can catch more marshmallows on her bracelets. A fun addition is to have someone make a sound effect for each hit—"Pow!" or "Bang!"

Jeff Mattesich

Wish We Wore Velcro

Gather the students into a large circle, and have them take off their shoes. Create a big pile of shoes in the middle of the circle (be sure to mix them up). Have the students put their arms around each other (as in a huddle).

The object of the game is for the students to put their shoes back on without using their hands. This is a good team-building game because the circle members have to work together to accomplish the common goal. Have multiple teams go head to head or have the whole group go against the clock. *Mark Maines*

K-2

You need a large cargo net (you'll find other uses for the cargo net, guaranteed!), some rope, bolts, or rings in the walls or ceiling, lots of winter clothing from a thrift store, and an air horn or a prize that can be secured to the net.

Attach the cargo net to the ceiling or wall so it hangs down to the ground. Make sure it's secured to beams so it won't fall. Place the winter clothing in two piles in front of the net. Place the prize or horn at the top of the net.

Choose two contestants. (This game can be played many ways with classes or genders competing against each other.) To begin, the two players race to put on all the clothes (for example, snow bibs, gloves, ski masks, hats, scarves, etc.) When they have put on all the clothes, they race to the net and climb for the prize. Whoever reaches the top first wins.

Melissa Dickinson

Yeah or Nay

You need a video camera, video-editing capabilities, a willing volunteer, and a public place to interview strangers.

Take the video camera out to a public place (a local college is usually the best). Have a list of tasks you'll ask people to do, such as army-crawling through the fountain, eating a goldfish, or hitting a stranger with a whipped-cream pie. Ask random people to do a task, let them answer, and then watch them try to do it (while taping the whole process). Edit the tape so it can be paused after the question is asked or after the answer is given.

Show the first clip to the students. Ask a student to guess if the person on the tape will be able to complete the task. (Does the person appear to have the guts to do it or not?) Then show the second clip to see if the student was correct. Give a prize for a correct guess. You can also have two volunteers put point wagers on each clip and play it like a game show.

Melissa Dickinson

Worst-Case Scenarios

Check out www.worstcasescenarios.com, or the board game or book, and pull questions regarding disaster situations. Have four volunteers come up on stage, and ask each a question. If she gets it wrong (which she will because the questions are ridiculous), she must perform a physical, mental, or culture challenge. She gets to choose which kind of challenge she wants to do. (Sounds like the old show *Double Dare*.)

Examples of physical challenges are shooting a spit wad through a straw using only one nostril, eating a hot pepper, or doing 15 pushups. Mental challenges are things like reciting the Pledge of Allegiance, reciting the multiplication table for the number eight, or naming the capitals of certain states. Culture challenges are things like naming three of Shakespeare's plays, doing an interpretive dance to the Barney theme song, or improvising a made-up love poem to the guy sitting in the front row. As long as a contestant either answers a Worst Case Scenario question right or completes a challenge, he stays in the game. If he misses a question or a challenge, he is out. It makes it more interesting if each student contestant is the representative for her grade and the whole grade gets a prize if its rep wins.

Chris Carter

The World's Slowest Race

Divide your group into two teams. Give each team a balloon and a baseball cap. The first person in each line must walk to a specific spot while balancing the balloon on the baseball cap, then turn around and tag the next person in line. If any other part of their body touches the balloon, they must start over.

NOTE—Don't make the space they have to walk too long. About 15 feet will do.
Steve Case

Tallest Tower

Once your group plays this simple game, your students will request it over and over. You need a large number of empty soda pop cans and bags of large marshmallows. Don't use the mini ones.

Divide your group into teams of equal numbers and give each team a pile of soda cans and a few bags of marshmallows. When you say, "Go," each team tries to build the tallest tower of cans. At the same time, the teams can throw marshmallows at other teams' towers to try to knock them over.

Set a time limit. The team with the tallest tower at the end of the time wins. Teams can assign certain duties, such as stacker, blocker, and thrower.   *Steve Case*

Bound and Giggled

Divide your group into pairs. Tie pairs together with yarn, right wrist to right wrist and left wrist to left wrist. Do the same with ankles and elbows. Leave enough slack so they can move. Set up an obstacle course, and watch the fun. *Steve Case*

Musical Water

Play this game outside or in a room that can be mopped easily. Have your group sit in a circle, and give each student a paper cup filled with water. Before you fill the cups, mark one cup with an *X*. When the music starts, the group begins passing the cups around the circle to each other. When the music stops, the person holding the *X* cup is out of the game.

Here's the catch—the person holding the X cup is out, but the X cup stays in the game. The same number of water cups remains regardless of how many teens are left in the circle. Have pitchers of water or a hose on hand to refill spilled cups.

Steve Case

Parameters

Tell your students they must walk around the outside of the entire building. The catch is that they must keep one hand on the building at all times, even if they have to crawl over hedges or stairs. You can set up extra obstacles before you begin. This game can also be played on the interior of a building. *Steve Case*

Cooperation Competition

For this game, teams consist of two people. You can have just a few people participate, or you can include the whole group. Have as many two-person teams as you want. You'll need the following bag of supplies for each team.

1. A shoe with the laces removed. Put the laces in the bag.
2. One section of a newspaper and a rubber band
3. A small container of Play-Doh
4. Three Oreo cookies
5. A needle and thread
6. A piece of 8.5 x 11 paper

Have the teams sit on the floor beside each other. For the competition, team members use the hand that is not next to their partner. One team member uses his right hand, and the other uses her left hand. When you say, "Go!" each team dumps the contents of its bag and completes the list of tasks.

1. Lace and tie the shoe.
2. Roll the newspaper and put the rubber band around it.
3. Make a cross out of the Play-Doh.
4. Twist the Oreo cookies apart and lick the icing off.
5. Thread the needle.
6. Make a paper airplane, but don't throw it.
7. Stand up when you finish all of the tasks.

Award points as they finish. For a bonus round, see whose paper airplane flies the best. *Alex Roller*

Amazon Women

Ask all the boys to sit or stand in a group with their arms linked together. Ask the girls to surround them in a large circle. The girls try to pull the boys out of the group by (almost) any means necessary. Set a time limit. The girls get points for every guy they pull out of the group.

Pocket Scavenger Hunt

Put students in teams of 8 to10, and go on a scavenger hunt. In this version, students search for the items you ask for, but only in their pockets, wallets, and purses. The first team whose runner brings an item or items to the front of the room gets the points for that round. Remember, points are free, so give them away, well, freely! Here are some suggestions for possible items. *Alex Roller*

- 1975 quarter
- movie ticket stub from last weekend
- five different shoes tied together and still on your feet (all five people must come up)
- two rings tied on a shoelace—not on the shoe

- a Visa card
- 43 cents in pennies
- four belts attached together
- student IDs from three different schools
- a sock on the outside of a shoe
- someone who can name all Seven Dwarves

When the Roll is Called up Yonder

You'll need a few cases of toilet paper for this game. You can play this game with as few as four or as many as 20 students, depending on how much toilet paper you have.

Separate your group into teams. When you say, "Go!" each team builds a stack of toilet paper rolls as high it can. Provide chairs or let students sit on one another's shoulders to reach the high points. For added fun set a time limit of 20 seconds or so.
Ken Lane

Sing Me a Song

Get four groups to compete against each other with not more than five people in each group. The host chooses three words for this game. The groups have 10 seconds to come up with a song containing the first word. If the team doesn't start singing within the 10 seconds, it's eliminated. If the team does come up with a song, the host moves on to the next team. Then, the next team must come up with a song containing that word. The word doesn't change until a team gets eliminated. Once a team is eliminated, the host randomly selects the next team to start off with the new word.

Melissa Dickinson

Hanger 18

This game is as much fun to watch as it is to play. You need some sturdy, hard, plastic coat hangers. (Do NOT use the wire hangers: you could poke somebody's eye out. Make sure the hangers are smooth, so students' heads don't get scratched.) Ask for two volunteers. Spread the hangers so they fit snugly over the students' heads with the hook facing off the side of the head toward the opponent.

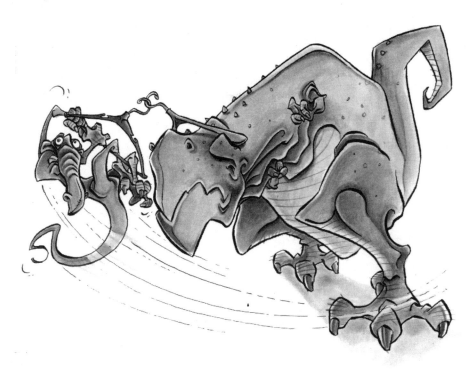

The object of the game is to pull the hanger from the other person's head by using only the hook of one's own hanger. Players are not permitted to touch each other during the game. Be careful how often you play this game. Your church may start noticing an epidemic of deformed and broken hangers.

Brad Sorenson

Pore Strip Relay

Break the students into any size relay teams. Have each team select a student to wear the pore strip. This student's head is wrapped in wide masking tape with the sticky side out. Leave an opening for breathing and seeing. Place a flat bowl with unpopped popcorn kernels at the other end of the room. Give each team an empty container.

Then send the taped student to the other end of the room and see how many kernels he can stick to his head without using his hands. He must rub his head in the bowl, then run back so the team can remove the kernels from the strip and put them in the empty container.

The object is to be the most efficient team to clean out their friend's pore strip. Repeat as many times as possible in the specified time. The team with the most kernels at the end wins. It is easiest to weigh each container to determine a winner.

Mike Arzie

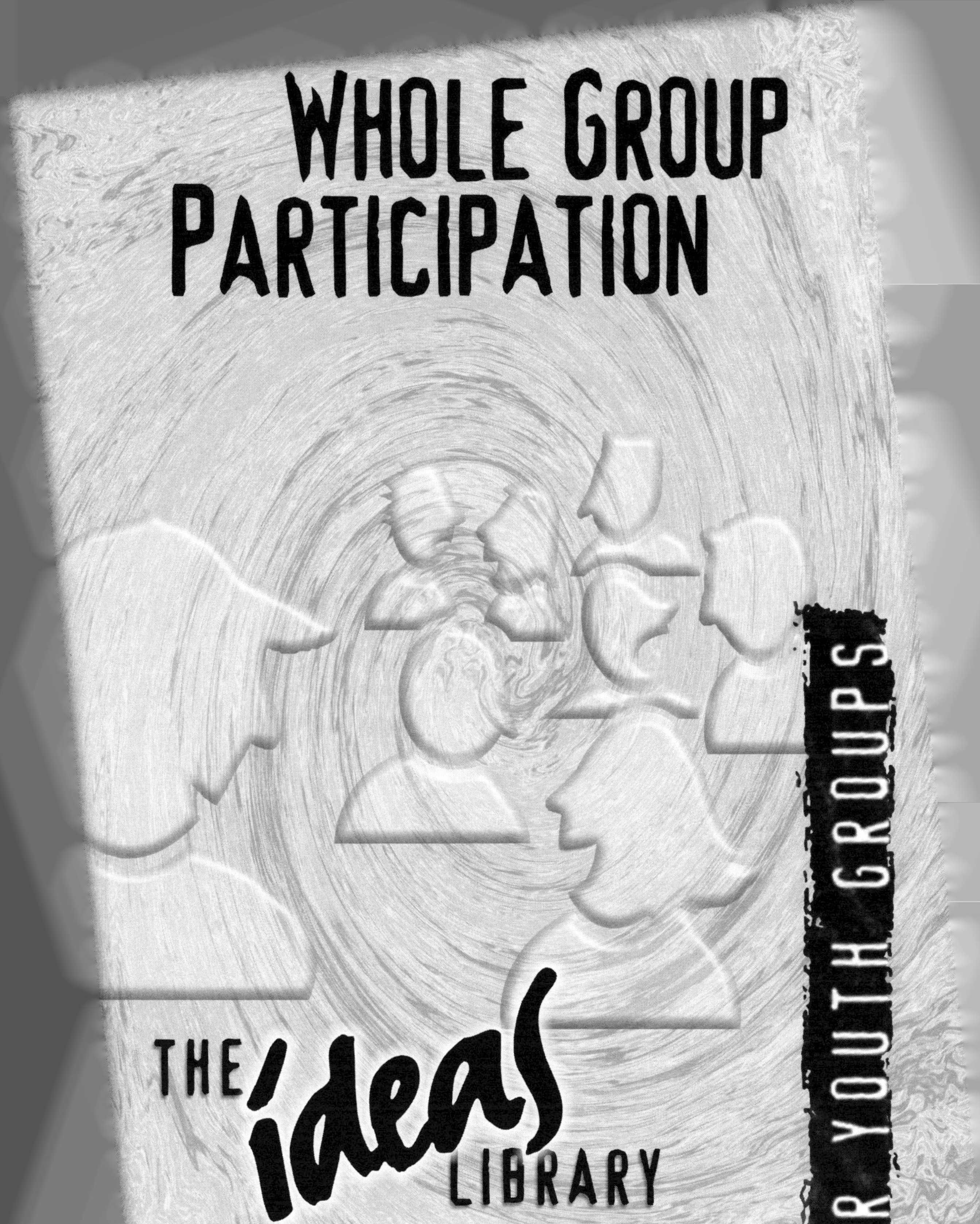
WHOLE GROUP
PARTICIPATION
THE ideas LIBRARY
R YOUTH GROUPS

What Do Boys Know?
(or What Do Adults Know?
or What Do Girls Know?)

You need a video camera, video-editing capabilities, a willing volunteer, and a public place to interview strangers.

Take the camera to a public place (a local college is usually the best), and have a list of questions to ask boys and men at random regarding women's lives, history, and issues. (Some examples include—*What do you call a manicure for your toes?* or *What is the name of the woman on the* We can do it! *poster?*) Ask three men the same question. When you edit the video, show the host asking the question and then put up a tri-split screen with each guy's face on it and his name under his face. Pause the tape at this point in each round. Prepare six to eight scenarios for a good game.

Roam around the room to get volunteers. Show each volunteer the first clip of the question and then the three faces. The volunteer decides which one got it right, if no one did, or if they all did. Award a prize for each correct answer.

Melissa Dickinson

How Clowns Do It

You need duct tape, Hula Hoops, and a plastic trash can. Make shapes on the ground with the duct tape, and see how many students can cram into the space. They must all be inside the tape; any part of the body on the tape disqualifies. Students should get creative and put other students on their backs, etc.

Repeat the same idea and have them cram into Hula Hoops, trashcans, under tables, and whatever else you can think of. You can have multiple stations in one room with teams running between each one (give each station a name and then make up a checklist). That way they're not only trying to do some crazy acrobatics, but they are trying to do them quickly so their team wins.

Jeff Mattesich

Search for the Snap

Before your group meets, take 15 or so pictures of things around your church. Take the pictures so the subject matter isn't recognizable instantly. For example, take a close-up picture of the top of the pulpit, a picture of a hinge on one of the main doors, and the trashcan in your office. The options are limitless.

Give each team a copy of each picture (or color photocopy them onto one sheet), and give them 15 minutes to find as many of the picture spots as possible. Tally points for the most spots found, and reward the winning team by taking a group picture of them and putting it on the bulletin board. *Jenny Mattesich*

Reverend Finger Paint

Divide your group into teams. Roll out six-foot sheets of butcher paper and give one to each team. Tell them they have 10 minutes to finger paint a portrait of the senior pastor.

VARIATION—Get your senior pastor involved in this by having him lie down on the paper sheets to be traced prior to the game. Also have the pastor's spouse be the judge.

Steve Case

It's Raining on Your Picnic

Give groups of students a plastic picnic tablecloth for each group. Take them outside and have each group gather around its tablecloth, holding the sides. Have staff members toss water balloons while the students try to catch the balloons in the tablecloths. Give teams 100 points for each unbroken balloon at the end of the game.

VARIATION—This game is a lot more fun if you have your adults on the church roof, throwing the balloons down. But be sure the adults want to play the game and not just nail students with balloons.   *Jenny Mattesich*

Who's Not Here?

This game is great when a lot of the students don't know the names of the rest of the group. You need a very large box (a large appliance box from behind a mall or other store works well), a blanket, and two volunteers to hold the blanket while members of Team 1 hide in the box.

To begin divide the students into teams of about 10 students each. Choose one group to start in position 1. Place a blanket on the floor so that teams 2, 3, or 4 can see who's in Team 1 and memorize their names. After a minute or so, the two blanket holders raise the blanket as members of Team 1 (a few, some, or as many as will fit) crawl into the box. Not all of Team 1's members have to get in the box. Some may still stand outside it.

Now choose one of the other three teams to recite the names of Team 1's members who are hidden in the box. The blanket holders drop the blanket to the floor, and the guessing team has 30 seconds to identify who's missing. When a team correctly identifies who's hidden in the box, they change places with Team 1. Of course, the highest number of "recalled names" wins the day. The students learn one another's names and have a blast getting scrunched into the box together. *Tim Bilezikian*

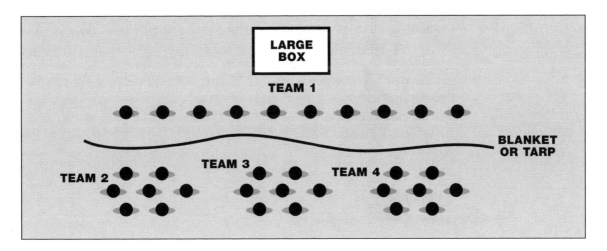

Pit

Have everyone split into groups of 8 to 10. Then select a theme that some, but not all, of the people in the group will share, such as birth month, color of clothing, eye color, shoe brand, or number of letters in first name. When you say, "Pit's open!" the groups begin trading their members.

They can trade any number of people at one time with any other group, but the traded members must all share the common theme. For instance, if the theme is birth month, a team may trade two *Februarys* at the same time, but not a *February* and a *March*. Teams make trades by yelling the number of members they want to trade and finding another group that is yelling the same number. This works best if the groups are situated in a circle, but it could be hilarious if groups move around freely.

Once a group has eight members with the same theme, they yell "Come on _____!" (whatever theme they share). Each win is worth 10 points. To continue the game, assign a new theme and open the pit again.   *David Rydman*

Bomb Squad

Set a timer for as long you want (10 to 15 minutes is a good length). Hide the timer somewhere in the building. The person who finds the bomb *before* it goes off wins (The winner gets to hide the bomb for the next round). For larger groups play the game outdoors, and set the timer for a longer time.   *Stephanie Pearce*

Elephants in the Dark

This is one of those more-the-merrier games. You need a strobe light and a room that you can make completely dark. Come up with five or six different animals that can be mimicked easily (giraffes are not a great choice). Write the animals' names on index cards, one animal per card, until you have about 6 to 10 cards for each animal, depending on the size of your group.

Choose an adult volunteer who is a ham to demonstrate the various ways each animals should be mimicked. Have the students walk around the room and link up with the other animals in their herd. Students must not speak. They can only make animal noises. Give them three to five minutes. Just before they begin, turn off the lights and hit the strobe!   *Joel Lusz*

Glow for It

This one takes a little prep work, but the result is worth it. Spray paint some Hula Hoops and beach balls with glow-in-the-dark paint (or use white hoops and balls and hook up some black lights). Suspend the Hula Hoops from the ceiling and have students try to throw the balls through the hoops in the dark.

Designate certain hoops for specific teams or make it a free-for-all. It is difficult to keep score because the whole room is dark, but it's a whole lot of fun.
                                                           Jenny Mattesich

True Colors

Have a month-long color war between grades. Give each grade its own team color.

Then give points for every item that teams bring to youth group meetings week in their color, including clothing and other objects. Keep a running tally, create color-themed games.

VARIATIONS—Give teams 20 sheets of paper in their color to create paper planes. Have everyone throw them all at the same time, and the color that goes t farthest wins. Make gross shakes of food items in each team's color and have contest to see which team drinks their down first. Give each team 100 toothpick and their own color of Play-Doh. The team that builds the highest sculpture wins

Jenny Mattesich

Something's on the Ceiling

All you need is a bunch of students, some masking tape, and a wall that's at least 20 feet tall. Use this game as a great crowdbreaker or team-building exercise.

Divide the group into teams of 5 or 10 players, and give each team some duct tape. The goal is to get the tape to stick on the wall as high as possible while working together as a group. Sounds kind of stupid, but they'll love it.

Play this in a safe place, and lay down the ground rules ahead of time: no standing on shoulders and no jumping off of the wall to get higher. But students can use anything on their persons and their bodies. We've had tape as high as 30 feet on the wall because a group thought through the problem and worked together.

Heath Kumnick

American Idle

Everybody gets to play this one. In fact, you may want to start with the youth leader. Choose a couple of students who can take some ridicule because this one will bring out the laughs. Play a song through headphones to the chosen student who has the lyrics in hand. They sing the words, but the audience cannot hear the music—just the tone-deaf singing. Have the rest of the group vote on who does the best job. For extra fun, video tape the singers and play them all back at once. *JD*

I Lost My Marbles

You need chairs for everyone and tons of glow-in-the-dark super balls. (You can find these on the Internet at www.ustoy.com.)

Seat the students in rows (if you have a large group) or in two long lines (if you have fewer than 50 students). Divide the super balls in half and put a box in front of each section or row.

Turn off all the lights so the balls glow, and set the timer for about three minutes. Dump all of the balls in front of the first students in each row. Their job is to pass all of the balls to the back of their lines by pushing them under their seats and behind them.

Once the balls get to the back, the students there toss them forward until they're in the front row again. The section with the most super balls back in the box when time is up wins. *Melissa Dickinson*

Rocket Launch

You need lots of foam finger rockets (www.recfx.com is a good source), a fish net, about 12 feet of PVC pipe, duct tape, and two pairs of goggles (or catcher's gear). Divide the pipe into two 6-foot sections (or less depending on the height of the room). Duct tape a fish net to the end of each pipe and place the protective gear on two volunteers—one guy and one girl.

When both volunteers are fully guarded by protective gear, give them the fish net and pipe. Distribute the rockets throughout the audience. The girls shoot at their girl volunteer's net and guys aim for the guy's net. The team that catches the most rockets in the net wins. You can also play this game by pitting grades against each other. *Melissa Dickinson*

Strobe Light Volleyball

This is an excellent indoor game for large groups in a large room, especially during rainy weather. Divide the group into two teams. Set up a volleyball net or bed sheet so the top of the net is approximately five feet above the floor. Tell the players to sit down on their team's side of the net with their legs crossed. From this position play a regular game of volleyball with the following changes.

Adrienne Cali

1. Use a small beach ball.
2. Use hands and head only (no feet).
3. Make all serves overhand from the center of the group.
4. Because each player has limited mobility, use more participants (20 to 25 per team).
5. Use a strobe light.
6. Apply all other volleyball rules.

From the Book of Bubbles

Provide bubble solution and bubble wands for each person in the group. Or use the world's greatest bubble solution recipe found at

www.bubbles.org/html/solutions/formulae.htm

and provide a variety of things to blow bubbles with.

Have students find favorite Bible passages and substitute certain words for the word *bubbles* (1 Corinthians 13 is a killer).

Each time the reader says the word *bubbles* the entire room blows as many bubbles as they can in five seconds. When all is done, make a Bible study of the passage you chose.

Steve Case

One Balloon, Two Balloon; Red Balloon, Blue Balloon

You need masking tape and at least two balloons per player.

The object of this game is to have the fewest number of balloons on your side when the allotted time is up (15 to 40 minutes).

Place a line of tape down the center of the room to divide it in half. Then divide your group into two teams. Put an equal number of balloons on each side of the tapeline, and instruct your group that they have three minutes to get all of the balloons on the other side of the tapeline while the other team tries to do the same thing at the same time. Tell your students that they must hit the balloons continually. (Otherwise, some may see a loophole in the rules and try to hold as many balloons as they can until the end.)

After students play a round or two of this, they should be familiar with how the game works. At this point, they ought to be ready for a variation or two.

Jason Wetherholt

VARIATIONS—
1. Assign a different point value to each balloon color. For example—Yellow = 1, Orange = 2, Green = 3, Red = 4, Blue = 5. To make the game even more interesting, include one beach ball and make it worth 10 points. (If you use this variation, hang a poster on the wall that shows the colors and their corresponding point values. This is an excellent opportunity to include one or two of your artistic students.)
2. Play a series of three, five, or seven rounds.
3. Divide the room into four sections and use the same rules to play with four teams if your students begin to tire of the game (or if you have a large group).
4. If a balloon pops during play, the team that popped it is penalized the value of the balloon.
5. If you need to use up more time, have the students blow up the balloons at the beginning of the game.

Dominos Delivers

You can play this game with any number of people; it really gets people in a large group to mingle. Give everyone a domino when they enter the room, or use slips of paper that look like dominoes. The game gets students into groups quickly and sat down after the leader announces the directions. You'll think of endless possibilities, so have fun with it.   *Heath Kumnick*

Sample Directions

Get into groups with people who have the same domino.
Get into groups with people who have the same total of domino dots that you do.
Pair up with someone so that the total of your dominos equal 20.

Birds on a Statue

Play this game outside or in a large empty room. Make a circle on the floor with chalk or masking tape. The circle should be just a little smaller than it needs to be to hold your whole group. (The circle represents the top of the statue.) Create a larger circle around the center circle to represents the flight path. Play music and have students walk around outside the outer circle with their arms out as if they're pigeons. When the music stops, all the pigeons must land on the statue. Someone is going to get crowded out. The last person to land gets a point but is not out of the game. Play as many rounds as the group wants.   *Steve Case*

So what killer crowd breaker have you invented lately?

Are your kids still talking about that mixer you invented for last month's meeting or party? Youth Specialties pays $40 (and in some cases, more) for unpublished, field-tested ideas that have worked for you.

You've probably been in youth work long enough to realize that sanitary, theoretical, tidy ideas aren't what in-the-trenches youth workers are looking for. They want—*you* want—imagination and take-'em-by-surprise novelty in meetings, parties, and other events...ideas that have been tested and tempered and improved in the very real, very adolescent world you work in.

So here's what to do:

• Sit down at your computer, get your killer crowd breaker out of your head and onto your hard drive, then e-mail it to ideas@youthspecialties.com
Or print it off and fax it to 619-440-0582 (Attn: Ideas)
•If you need to include diagrams, photos, art, or samples that help explain your crowd breaker, stick it all in an envelope and mail it to our street address: Ideas, 300 South Pierce Street, El Cajon, CA 92020.
•Be sure to include your name and all your addresses and numbers.
•Let us have about three months to give your idea a thumbs up or down*, and a little longer for your 40 bucks.

* Hey, no offense intened if your idea isn't accepted. It's just that our fussy Ideas Library editor has these *really* meticulous standards. If the crowd breaker isn't creative, original, and just plain fun in an utterly wild or delightful way, she'll reject it (reluctantly, though, because she has a tender heart). Sorry. But we figure you deserve only the best ideas.

Resources from Youth Specialties

Ideas Library
Ideas Library on CD-ROM 2.0
Administration, Publicity, & Fundraising
Camps, Retreats, Missions, & Service Ideas
Creative Meetings, Bible Lessons, & Worship Ideas
Crowd Breakers & Mixers
Crowd Breakers & Mixers 2
Discussion & Lesson Starters
Discussion & Lesson Starters 2
Drama, Skits, & Sketches
Drama, Skits, & Sketches 2
Drama, Skits, & Sketches 3
Games
Games 2
Games 3
Holiday Ideas
Special Events

emergentys
Adventures in Missing the Point
The Emerging Church
Stories of Emergence

Help! Books
Help! I'm a Junior High Youth Worker!
Help! I'm a Small Church Youth Worker!
Help! I'm a Small-Group Leader!
Help! I'm a Sunday School Teacher!
Help! I'm an Urban Youth Worker!
Help! I'm a Volunteer Youth Worker!

Quick Question Books
Have You Ever...?
Name Your Favorite
Unfinished Sentences
What If...?
Would You Rather...?

StudentWare
Sex Has a Price Tag

Resources from Youth Specialties

Bible Curricula

Backstage Pass to the Bible Kit
Creative Bible Lessons from the Old Testament
Creative Bible Lessons in 1 & 2 Corinthians
Creative Bible Lessons in Galatians and Philippians
Creative Bible Lessons in John
Creative Bible Lessons in Romans
Creative Bible Lessons on the Life of Christ
Creative Bible Lessons on the Prophets
Creative Bible Lessons in Psalms
Wild Truth Bible Lessons
Wild Truth Bible Lessons 2
Wild Truth Bible Lessons-Pictures of God
Wild Truth Bible Lessons-Pictures of God 2
Wild Truth Bible Lessons-Dares from Jesus

Topical Curricula

Creative Junior High Programs from A to Z, Vol. 1 (A-M)
Creative Junior High Programs from A to Z, Vol. 2 (N-Z)
The Disciple Experiment
Girls: 10 Gutsy, God-Centered Sessions on Issues That Matter to Girls
Good Sex
Graceland
Guys: 10 Fearless, Faith-Focused Sessions on Issues That Matter to Guys
The Justice Mission
Live the Life! Student Evangelism Training Kit
The Next Level Youth Leader's Kit
Roaring Lambs
So What Am I Gonna Do with My Life?
Student Leadership Training Manual
Student Underground
Talking the Walk
What Would Jesus Do? Youth Leader's Kit
Wild Truth Bible Lessons
Wild Truth Bible Lessons 2
Wild Truth Bible Lessons-Pictures of God
Wild Truth Bible Lessons-Pictures of God 2
Wild Truth Bible Lessons-Dares from Jesus